MINDING THE GAP

Choosing to Thrive in an Uncertain World

Rob Stones

MINDING *THE GAP*

Choosing to Thrive in an Uncertain World

First published 2022 by FutureShape Ventures.

Author: Rob Stones

Editor: Valerie Stones

Copyright to this work is asserted by Rob Stones of FutureShape Ventures.

No portion of this book may be reproduced or printed without permission.

ISBN: 978-0-646-85453-3
©FutureShape Ventures, 2022. All Rights Reserved.

For other publications by Rob Stones visit www.futureshape.com.au

*This book is dedicated to the memory of
Dr William Glasser M.D.
Dr Glasser was a visionary whose insights and inspiration showed me,
and millions of other people, how to enhance our own well-being and
personal freedom.*

and to

*The work of my colleagues in the Glasser Institute in Australia, and in
associated Institutes across the globe.
Thank you for everything I have learned from you,
and for your commitment to teaching
Choice Theory to the world.*

MINDING THE GAP
Choosing to Thrive in an Uncertain World

Rob Stones

Table of Contents

Prelude: The Quest for Certainty	1
Section 1: The Gap	**6**
1. Living in the Gap	7
2. Tea or Coffee	13
3. Brain and Mind	18
4. How the 'Habit Brain' Learns	26
5. Our Genetic Needs	31
Section 2: Managing the Gap	**38**
6. A Pivotal Choice - To be in Control	39
7. Choosing to give up Control	47
8. The Limits of Choice	54
9. 'Wants' - Our Internal Reference Points	60
Section 3: Narrowing the Gap	**69**
10. The World we Experience	70
11. Avoidance Motivation	79
12. Behave yourself!	86
Section 4: Shaping the Gap	**94**
13. Relationships and the Brain	95
14. Finding Fault	103
15. Choosing Misery?	112
16. The Challenge of Emotions	122
17. Desirable Doubt	134
Section 5: Thriving in the Gap	**142**
18. Is What I Am Doing Helping Me?	143
19. Happiness and 'the Good Life'	150
20. Ingredients of 'the Good Life'	161
21. Minding the Gap	173
22. A Meaningful Life	183

"Those who do not observe the movements of their own minds must of necessity be discontented."

Marcus Aurelius

"The mind is difficult to control; swiftly and lightly, it moves and lands wherever it pleases. It is good to tame the mind, for a well-tamed mind brings happiness."

The Dhammapada (Ancient Buddhist Scripture) verse 35

Prelude

The Quest for Certainty

That we live in an uncertain world is certain – one of the few things that we can all be sure of! To be human is to draw daily breath in a world over which we have only a little control. We aspire to be happy and for our lives to be meaningful, though neither is guaranteed. As the author of 'Ecclesiastes' wisely reminded us: "Time and chance happen to all"[1]

Choice is a pervasive feature of this unpredictable experience.

At every moment, whatever is happening around us; whatever we are doing, thinking, or feeling; we choose 'what next'.

Whether we are happy or discontented, our choices played a part in getting us here. Whether through intention or consequence, by accident or design, we navigated to our present circumstance by choosing. The possibility of changing or improving the future depends on choice. Choices present themselves to us from our entry into life until our exit. As long as we are breathing, each choice we make has some implications for the next.

---

[1] Old Testament: Ecclesiastes 9:11

None of us can avoid the implications of our choices. We choose to take or miss opportunities, to avoid pain or to embrace it. We make decisions deliberately or impulsively. If our choices have a desirable result, we claim ownership. If we don't like where they lead us, we often excuse ourselves with: "I had no choice!".

However we think about our choices, whether we take responsibility for them or not, they assemble the framework of our life and are instruments of the way we regard ourselves. Though we plan as best we can to hold the world still for our convenience, it only rarely cooperates. When things don't work out, we can flourish or despair, thrive nimbly despite happenstance or stumble on our way. These are choices.

Choices and our Synaptic Self

Every time we choose one thing over another we create - or strengthen - a chain of connections between the neurons[2] in our brain. Every time we make the same choice, these pathways of neurological sequence become stronger, more established.

It's a little like watching the rain create channels in an untouched sandy slope. The streams of water soon find pathways through the more receptive areas of the terrain. Very soon shallow channels are established. The more the water flows through these channels, the deeper they become. The fragile grooves worn into the sand soon become rivulets that are easily found by the water from each new downpour.

The brain, almost as malleable at our birth as the unmarked sandy slope, is similarly patterned by the choices we make, soon settling into familiar pathways. As choice is built upon choice, the behaviours that result become our habits – our familiar and preferred way of doing things.

---

[2] Specialised nerve cells that transmit impulses.

The Quest for Certainty

Each choice that we make has an influence on future choices. At any point in our lives, the synaptic connections that we have already made provide receptive pathways for our new decisions. Established preferences create the tendencies to think and act in ways with which we are familiar. Every new choice is either limited by, or enabled by, the courses we chose in the past.

We all begin creating the person we become as adults from the very first options we choose. In our earliest years, many of our choices were made unconsciously – long before we had either the capacity or the awareness to be deliberate. By the time we become conscious of 'choosing', we already have innumerable established pathways.

The Construction of Self

Even as our awareness emerges and deliberation and reflection become part of our lives, we do make many choices automatically: the result of already well-established channels of brain activity. It's a little as if we begin constructing ourselves years before we had any sense of the person we are becoming. Almost accidentally, the 'self 'we have become was constructed by choices.

Imagine if you were to build a house this way, assembling it from whatever materials were to hand: perhaps putting up the roof first to keep the rain off and only later trying to add a foundation; adding doors and windows wherever they were needed for light or passage. I am guessing it would be a difficult enterprise and result in a rickety structure!

Now you may think that I am suggesting that much of our life is 'determined' by our early experience, leaving us blindly following the established pathways in our brain. That's certainly how some people feel. It can seem that way. But there is an alternative narrative, one that explains how we can expand the boundaries of our personal freedom through choices. We can enhance our ability to be powerful and fulfilled; take on a perspective that encourages us to renovate and rebuild rather than put up with how things are. By taking control of our choices, we can learn energising practices with which to navigate the episodes of our living, rather than trudge through the inevitable passages of our days.

The sandy slope metaphor I have used to explain the way the brain constructs itself is apposite - but limited. It's true, but it's not the whole truth. There is a far more complete explanation of the role that choices play in our lives that is emancipating and enabling. With different knowledge, the ability to act consciously, and the will to learn new skills, we can use our present and future choices to re-design both whom we are and who we will become.

Mind: The X Factor

In the much more complete account, the way our brain automates our choices is only part of the story. Each of us is a mind as well as a brain. From the neural energy of the brain emerges mind: a conscious self-organising capacity that can direct and alter the activity of the brain. Self-organisation is the wild spirit of the self, the capacity that liberates us from the machinery of brain and invites us to recreate ourselves intentionally.

The mind offers us the ability to manage the sandy landscape of our habits - to build dams and divert channels in the sandy slope. Well-established streams of unconscious activity can be redirected, guiding the flow of living in new directions.

The mind provides us with our slower thinking[3], the ability to be purposeful and goal-directed. With awareness, we can decide where the tributaries of thought and action flow. When we understand and learn to use the mind's capacity, we also learn how to manage the hidden torrents of the unconscious. We can introduce diversions and detours in the landscape of habit, nudge ourselves towards new courses – or reverse direction and seek different destinations.

---

[3] As described by Daniel Kahneman in 'Thinking, Fast and Slow', 2011.

The Quest for Certainty

Who we are now is the product of our past choices.

Who we are becoming is a matter of present and future choice.

These pages describe some of the ways that options are presented to us through our human operating system; ways to understand and take charge of our mind's processes. Through these choices, we can learn new ways to tend and guide the neural connections that choreograph each step in the dance of life.

As we come to understand that we are owners and operators of a personal mental control system, we can become composers of our own future; resilient responders to the challenge of a reality in which certainty is a scarce commodity.

Section 1: The Gap

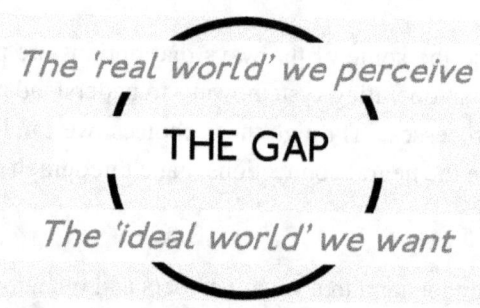

*"Between stimulus and response there is a space.
In that space is our freedom and power to choose a response.
In our response lies our growth and our happiness."*

Victor Frankl

*"Choice Theory explains that, for all practical purposes,
we choose everything we do."*

William Glasser

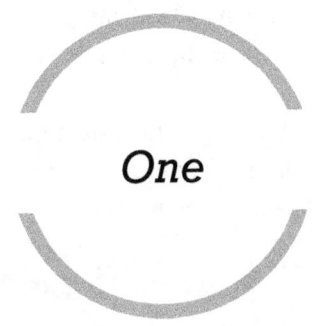

One

Living in 'the Gap'

Living in 'The Gap'

We all live our lives in *the Gap*[1] between 'the real' and our ideal. On the stage of life, *the Gap* is the backdrop against which we make our choices.

Whoever we are and whatever we are doing, this comparison between 'how things are' and 'how we would like them to be' is an abiding constant. Although we are not always aware of it, *the Gap* is ever-present.

Every day we choose the thoughts and actions that we believe will narrow *the Gap* - that will lead to more of what we want in life. In our attempts to feel 'in control' - to be the willing architects of our own well-being - our choices are the tools with which we shape our individuality and strive for achievement and fulfilment.

---

[1] Because *the Gap* between our perceptions and our desires is the recurrent theme of this book, this space between the real and the ideal will usually be presented as *the Gap* whenever I refer to it.

And because pain and the threat of suffering are an inevitable part of living, we make choices that we hope will avoid or minimise discomfort.

It is very rare for us to sustain the sense that things are completely 'right' for any length of time. *The Gap* is our inescapable inheritance, the dubious gift bestowed on us by our humanity - by the ways in which our brain is wired.

Whether our *Gaps* are huge or tiny, they create an itch that we are constantly scratching as we try to make the best of our lives.

Acceptance or Resentment?

Now, I am not telling a sad story. It's simply how things are. *The Gap* is the paradoxical source of our motivation and the facilitator of personal growth. Nevertheless, attitudes and beliefs about this difference between the reality of life and the idyll we desire vary widely. Some of us just accept that it is 'just what is'. We say to ourselves something like: "Life was never meant to be perfect" and manage our circumstances through the best choices we can make. *The Gap* is always there, but because we expect it, we accept it. Because we accept it, we learn to manage it.

Of course, even those of us who are relatively sanguine about this everyday divide between the actual and the ideal become dispirited at times. When *the Gap* becomes intrusive, when the present reality seems

Living in 'the Gap'

painfully incompatible with what we wish we were experiencing, we are all tempted to rail against 'the slings and arrows of outrageous fortune'![2] In the face of tragedy or oppression, even the most accepting of us push back against the threat or hurt we feel.

However, many people are ever conscious of this space between the real and the wanted. They resent it. They come to believe that life is unfair; that their circumstances are somehow cheating them out of the state of contentment that they feel they deserve. However small the divide between the quality of life they yearn for, and their perception of how things are, they notice it. Awareness of *the Gap* becomes pervasive. It's easy to become more than a little miserable if you experience life like that!

Even though it may seem a harsh feature of human design, whether you accept *the Gap* or resent it, the prospect of any different experience of life is non-existent. Whether we tolerate it or hate it, there is no escape from the urge to balance what's happening with what we want. It's the 'Catch-22' of our humanity that *the Gap* is inevitable. We need it in order to function!

The Gap Presents Choices

Because we are persons, human organisms with a mental control system, *the Gap* is intrinsic to our motivation. Everything we do comes from weighing our present experience against how we want things to be, and then behaving in order to reduce the difference. We are only occasionally doing this consciously or reflectively, but our brain activity is always pursuing its imperative – to protect and serve us by adjusting *the Gap*. Whether consciously or unconsciously, we are always making choices: seeking a way to behave that will bring our experience of life closer to one or another detail of our personal ideal.

---

[2] William Shakespeare: Hamlet, Act III Scene 1.

We have not evolved or been created to be lotus eaters. An idyllic life would rob us of the impulse to learn and grow. *The Gap* provides us with problems to solve and choices to make. It is the source of all our motivation and growth.

Choosing, then, is the ubiquitous activity of the mind. Comparing our present circumstances with our preferred ideal - and selecting a response - is our constant companion as we weave our pathway through life. We are shaped by the choices we make as we respond to *the Gap*. The different ways in which we see the world and the diverse choices we make individuate us and distinguish us from other humans. No person is a clone of another. The permutations of choice and experience are too great to permit sameness.

Who we are now, and the life we presently lead, are largely the consequence of choices made at some time in the past. Although genetics and circumstances play a role in moulding our life's journey, we are all shaped by the options we take in the face of the events and experiences that we encounter.

In the same way, who we will become, and the degree of well-being and freedom we will experience in the future, will be the result of choices we make now and in times ahead. *The Gap* may be our burden, but it also emancipates us. Because we always have choices, and will always need to make choices, our choices matter!

Do we Choose our Life?

Now it often does not seem like that. More than one person has told me: "If I were really choosing my life, it would not be like this!" – and in many ways, they are right. We are never offered the opportunity to start from the beginning and choose our ideal life. Instead, we are the accumulation of innumerable past choices; some made impulsively in childhood; some made in response to circumstances we are trying to escape; many made rather carelessly or from habit.

Living in 'the Gap'

However, because we are the sole operators of our mental processes, we can learn to exert greater control over where our mind takes us in the future. By increasing our awareness of how our brain and mind work together, we can learn to enhance our personal freedom and well-being. We can't tinker with the past. None of us can hop into a time machine that will take us back in order to change our personal history. We can only act in the present to influence the future. Nothing else is possible.

Knowledge is Power

As only a few of us are psychology professionals or brain scientists, we can feel helpless when we don't understand how our brain and mind are managing our experience. This book offers a glimpse of what we **can** do - an opportunity to understand enough about the working of the human control system to enable us to make informed choices for now and for the future. Knowing how our mind is working, and its relationship with the activity of the brain, opens up powerful avenues of self-determination.

Because I am neither an academic nor a psychology professional, the descriptions of the brain and the mind presented in these pages will be couched in a lay-person's language. My hope is that anything my writing lacks in scientific precision will be made up by being easily understood by the reader.

Like you, I am a user of the mind - a practitioner not an 'expert'. I strive to be an 'informed' user. I have read at least some of the 'instruction books' - or at least the parts of them that I understand. What I have learned about how to manage *the Gap* has been acquired through the sunlight and shadow of a normal life. The information I offer is intended to be useful, without the obfuscation of detail.

Through our common humanity, we may have inherited the restless frustrations created by *the Gap* that we face every day - that pesky sense that things could always be better. However, we are endowed with a mind that is capable of learning from experience. Understanding our own experience - and learning to use *the Gap* rather than be discouraged by it - can increase our contentment, our freedom, and our sense of control over our life.

Like it or not, our biological design offers options, but not without cost. Inheriting the mind of *homo sapiens* may offer the potential for wisdom; the opportunity to take charge of our life. It doesn't bring with it the promise of tranquillity.

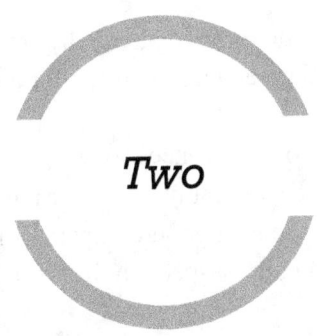

Tea or Coffee

"Would you like Tea or Coffee?"

I must have been asked that question hundreds of times. It's an example of the simplest kind of choice: would you like this or that? Technically this is described as a binary selection, like plus or minus: two things to choose between. What could be simpler?

And yet, when I think about how I give my answer to that simple question I realise that, in the space between the question and my answer, there is a lot going on.

Often my answer is automatic. If it's morning I prefer coffee; in the afternoon I will choose tea. I have long forgotten how I arrived at that preference, but now it seems right. My brain makes effortless connections to provide my habitual answer.

There are variations though. If I see that the coffee I am offered is 'instant', I will choose tea – but only if it's a 'normal' tea: 'English

Breakfast' or something equally traditional. In a choice between instant coffee and green tea, I will ask for a glass of water!

There are other nuances as well. If I have already had several cups of coffee, I will probably ask for tea, even if it is still morning. And after a pleasant dinner in good company, I might say 'yes' to a coffee to round off the evening – especially if it is accompanied by a small whisky!

The Mind in Action

What I have discovered is that even simple choices are not nearly as uncomplicated as they seem - and most of our choosing is far more complicated than: "Tea or Coffee?"

When we decide on a goal or a career; when we choose the beliefs we live by and the principles to teach to our children; when we choose whom to love or trust, all these difficult and important choices make a difference to our lives. Learning to choose the options that lead to opportunity and contentment while keeping ourselves safe is a life-long enterprise. Knowing what is actually happening in your mind when you are choosing is abundantly helpful. When we understand how our decisions are made, and how our choices are related to the circumstances of life, we can be far more in control and accepting than when we are ignorant of these processes.

The actual mechanism of individual choice is uncomplicated. As noted in the previous chapter it's based on making a comparison. We compare our perception of current circumstances with what we want, and then choose a behaviour to reduce the gap between the two. I like to present this through an image:

Tea or Coffee

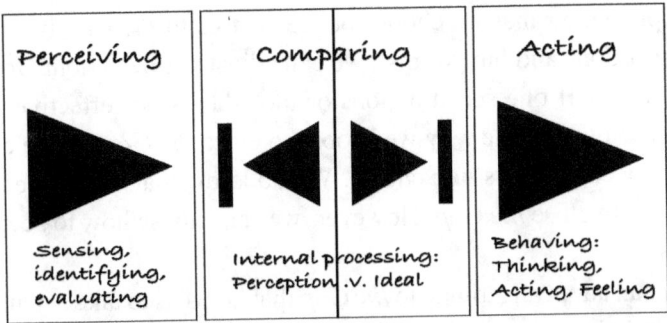

We take in information through our perceptual system. We compare the resulting perception to our 'wants': our ideal of how we would like things to be. We then generate a behaviour through which we intend to close *the Gap*.

There are four dimensions of our mental experience involved: our perceptions, our 'wants' (or ideal), a comparing process, plus the behaviour that we choose.

Understanding and managing each of these dimensions of our mental landscape provides us with the tools to prise open the gates to freedom and happiness:

- We can learn to manage our own perceptions of 'what's happening'. Realising that we are interpreters of our external experience and not passive recipients of sensory data gives us choices. It is liberating to know that we are active participants in the way we see the external world. We are doers, not 'done to'!
- Knowing how and why we create our 'wants' makes a critical contribution to our self-knowledge. These personal mental pictures or conceptions are assembled from the events, actions, and relationships that we have experienced as being satisfying and which we come to see as the 'ideal'. They are our own preferences, our personally created reference points. We can choose to modify them or replace them.

- Appreciating that we choose our responses to *the Gap* between our perceptions and our 'wants', we can adjust our behaviours to narrow *the Gap*. If one set of actions or thoughts is not effective, we can choose others. The **way** we choose to close *the Gap* can be effective or flawed, but it is **our** choice. We do know that we are genetically driven to close *the Gap*. However, we can choose how to accomplish this.
- We can adopt an attitude to *the Gap* that helps us to take a realistically optimistic approach to our own choices. While we pursue our 'wants', we can simultaneously manage our experience of the 'less than perfect' in order to thrive.

Choice and Responsibility

We will also tackle the central question of responsibility: can we really take charge of our choices or are we simply victims of our circumstances?

That takes us back to my choice of tea or coffee. If we make so many choices out of habit - or at least partly from our unconscious - are we really in control? Can we override the automatic selections made by the long-established synaptic connections in our brain? Is our sense that we are choosing just an illusion – our rationalisation of habituated brain pathways? Are we automatons, dabbling in the illusion of choice, or willing designers of our own life pathways?

A few minutes of scanning the media headlines or the themes of social media will quickly show us that many individuals seem to believe that their responses to people and events are 'caused' by circumstances beyond their control.

If they are right, then this book is irrelevant! If our past experiences and whatever happens outside ourselves determine our present and future, choice is an illusion. If our internal experience is created entirely by what's happening outside of us, then we are merely puppets misled by our minds and deluded by our illusion of control.

Tea or Coffee

These therefore are the pivotal questions:
- Are we in control of our choices – or controlled by circumstances?
- Is the apparent working of our mind merely a fictional narrative - or is it our internal perception of the human control system at work?
- Does our thinking provide us with a fanciful interpretation of our brain's neural activity - or do we really experience autonomy and choice?

These are big questions that will be explored in the pages that follow.

Three

Brain and Mind

Biological Brain with Constructed Mind

Are we the unwitting puppets of our biological brain, or is it possible to be the owners and originators of our actions? It's the critical question for a book about choices. Do we choose our actions and choices, or are we puppets following pathways pre-programmed into our genes or by our history?

On the first page of his seminal work 'Choice Theory'[1], William Glasser wrote: "For all practical purposes, we choose everything we do." Some people find that hard to accept. It implies too much responsibility. Surely there are things that we don't choose!

The first thing we have to accept is that we don't always choose the decisions we have to make! That sounds contradictory but it's not. Around us, other people and events collide and separate: the natural world is heaving with impenetrable patterns. Surrounded by this ever-evolving

---

[1] William Glasser, 'Choice Theory a New Psychology of Personal Freedom' Harper Collins 1998.

puzzle, we don't always get to choose the problems thrown our way by the fickleness of life. What we do get to choose is how to address these problems.

Another thing that can blinker our understanding of our choices is this. If we read the fine print of the human story, we might notice that all choices have consequences. It follows that we might choose a behaviour that has a painful consequence. Then when we focus on the **results** of our actions we say: "I didn't choose this!" – which is one reason why the unreflective may dismiss Glasser's assertion that we choose everything we do.

Glasser was right though. We do choose everything we do - both the behaviours that lead to pleasurable consequences and the ones that result in pain. And it's exactly because the effects of our choices can have such a profound influence on our life and our well-being that understanding the nature of choice is so helpful. The more we know about how the brain and the mind contribute to our choices, the more we can feel in control - not only of our choices but also of the consequences that flow from them.

Choosing is initiated by brain activity, which may be accompanied by a conscious mental process, but often is not. Patterns of brain activity 'notice' the disparity between our perception and the pleasurable feelings we desire. They then create the connections between brain cells that initiate a behaviour that will improve things. Our brain is always involved, but this activity in the cells and the connections in the brain does not always reach our mind. When they are conscious, our choices may be supported by reasoning. When they are unconscious, usually not!

From Brain comes Mind

For more than two thousand years the conventional view was that 'brain' and 'mind' are two ways of referring to the same thing. In normal conversation we often use 'Brain' and 'Mind' as if they were the same. If we differentiate at all we tend to think that mental activity is what the brain does – but it is a bit more complicated than that.

What the science of brain has revealed is this: activity in the brain generates bodily sensation. Think of it as a kind of aura of energy that results from the furious tumult of action and interaction among the vast number of connections in the brain. When this emanated energy reaches a certain intensity, it gives rise to awareness.[2] Initiated by the resonance of these bodily sensations, we have an internal perception, a conscious representation of our brain activity that is perceived by us as *symbolic* energy consisting of images and language.[3] The result of this energetic communication is that we have personal internal access to some of what is going on in our brain through thoughts and feelings. Our brain generates the vitality which we perceive as thought.

Even though the brain is sometimes described as if it is a fully-automated entity acting on its own, following familiar and pre-determined pathways, it's not. We have access to this machine! Our conscious thoughts and choices can sculpt and modify the brain's activity.

The 'Mind' that arises from the brain's activity is a self-organising system. Able to transform itself independently of its cerebral origins, the mind's processes can then loop back to modify or reorder the neural connections in the physical brain. Knowing this makes a huge difference to how we explain choosing to ourselves – and to the choices we can make.

---

[2] My very simplified interpretation of Antonio Damasio's explanation of the biological and emotional basis of human reasoning.
[3] "The human mind is a relational and embodied process that regulates the flow of energy and information within us." Dan Siegel: 'Mindsight' p52.

Brain and Mind

Mind Influences Brain

Realising that the exchange of energy between awareness and unconscious brain activity flows in both directions, we can come to understand how our conscious mind can change the activity of the 'habit brain'. Our mental processes emanate from the chemical and electrical activity of the brain, but then the conscious thoughts that result can influence and alter the way in which the brain itself works.

This is exciting! It's central to our ability to 'self-manage' - to use the reasoning powers of the mind to choose behaviours that are most likely to achieve the outcomes we want. We are not limited by our 'natural' brain reactions. We have the ability to influence and change our thinking and our actions – and even, as we will see, to regulate our emotions.

If it was unmodified by the mind, the brain would simply do what it has been designed to do: to protect and serve the body that it inhabits. Detecting danger, we would freeze, flee or fight. The most primitive centres of the brain have little subtlety. This automaticity is very useful when we are threatened with physical harm, but it also activates when we are faced with a social threat.[4]

Becoming angry in an instant when we suspect someone is talking down to us (a status threat) is 'natural' but often not useful. Our mental processes (experienced as thoughts) can help us manage that sudden flare of emotional energy and activate curiosity instead of hostility. We can think: "Why is this person talking to me like that?" instead of expressing anger.

Many children and some adults easily become angry or fearful. They react to what they believe is being 'done' to them. Not understanding that their

---

[4] David Rock's SCARF model illustrates the way in which threats to our Status, Certainty, Autonomy, Relationships and Fairness can instigate the same bodily response as does physical danger. 'SCARF: A Brain-Based Model for Collaborating with and Influencing Others' 2008

own mental processes play a part in interpreting what they perceive, they act on the apparent threat behind a look, a word, or a posture.

Choices that Improve our Lives

To make the best choices for ourselves in a complex social environment we need to choose our behaviours with more sophistication than the 'habit brain' provides. The 'quick and approximate' brain reaction may have served primitive humans. To thrive in the social world, we need the modifications that come from our conscious mind.

Let's examine specific examples of the beneficial way in which mind modifies brain. We might notice that the primitive brain tends to snatch: 'want something – take it'. Children (and some adults) tolerate no delay in acting to get what they want. The brain is designed to serve the organism by satisfying its desires in the immediacy of the present moment.

Without the awareness delivered by consciousness, the brain is organised to close *the Gap* between what we want and whatever is happening as fast as possible. When we feel hungry, our survival need prompts us towards finding food without delay. If we feel confined, imprisoned by circumstances or duty, our need for autonomy prompts us to find an impulsive solution in order to break free.

Without modification, the brain is not inclined to consider the long-term good of the person in whom it is embodied. Impulsivity is in our genes. However, having consciousness we can, and do, change that. The mind's capacity to remember past events and project them forward into new events allows us to consider the longer-term consequences of an act. We can weigh up the advantage of deferring gratification to a future time rather than closing *the Gap* immediately.

Over time, the mind's capacity to project into the future and learn from the past modifies the brain's directive system: the medial pre-frontal

Brain and Mind

cortex. This is the part of the brain that is used in planning. Located approximately behind the eyebrows, it is small in size but huge in importance. It can use the feedback from the mind to modify the way in which it sends orders to the rest of the brain. As it adapts, it learns that working towards a goal is more satisfying that instant gratification.

Delaying Gratification

This means that, over time, when our mind works out that waiting until we can prepare a healthy meal is preferable to buying fast food, the brain develops the habit of ignoring *the Gap* that's prompting us to grab a burger and chips. It means that our mind's decision to lose weight can inform the brain that short-term hunger is a good thing, not a threat. The slow but predictive action of the reflective mind loops back to make the changes that are needed in the brain.

Even more important is the mind's awareness that we sometimes need to tolerate an overbearing boss or spend a beautiful day studying indoors. With this insight, we can train the brain to ignore the impulse to tell the boss what we think of him or her - we need the job! We can suppress the frustration of forgoing a day at the beach in favour of the long-term benefits of gaining a qualification or skill.

This ability of the human organism to defer gratification is not 'built-in'. The brain may have a predisposition for planning in the structure of the pre-frontal cortex, but it needs the relationship with the mind to regulate and modify it.

It's impossible to overstate the significance of this for our well-being and survival. Imagine if, like a small child, we all wanted the toy or the cookie right now. If we took whatever we wanted, ate whenever we felt hungry, pushed aside whatever or whoever was in our way in order to close *the Gap*, we would find it difficult to live a satisfying life in the context of a social world. There are people like this. They lead unhappy lives. Many of them are imprisoned – either physically or psychologically. They seem unable to override their impulses. They may wish that things were different, but they have not learned how to defer a want.[5]

In these individuals, the reciprocal relationship between the mind and the brain that is needed to make a change in behaviour is not developed. Deliberate behaviour change is conceived in the mind and embedded in the brain's activity through repetition and success. Without these, the brain prompts us to take what we need - and the consequences be damned!

One Brain and Mind

Remember brain and mind are not two entities. Mind could not emerge apart from brain. They are a single aspect of self in two dimensions. They co-exist inside the container of skin that we call our body. It is the dance of this relationship, between the transmission of energy along nerve pathways and the awareness that arises from it, that enables us to learn and adapt so successfully. Through this relationship we are able to delay gratification, plan for long-term success and defer or modify our attempts to close *the Gap*. We are able to make similar modifications to many other products of mind and brain.

Armed with this capability, we lean towards choosing wisely for the long-term good of the organism we inhabit. We still feel the instant impulse to seize short-term satisfaction - I can never pass a doughnut without feeling temptation! - but we can learn to make the choices that lead to our long-term good.

Knowing this, we can develop the habit of self-management when we feel the attraction of impulse. The well-managed mind is able to ask: "Will

---

[5] With reliable parent modelling, most children learn to delay gratification quite naturally. They observe, and are coached to adopt, the habit of planning future pleasure through the exercise of patience, capability building and 'saving'. They learn to trust the promise that waiting will be worth it. The children of erratic or impulsive parents find it difficult to connect short term pain with long term achievement. As a result, much of what is expected of them at school makes little sense to them.

Brain and Mind

this make things better or worse?"; "Will I be happy with that choice or regret it later?"; "What do I really want in these circumstances?"

We can create the disposition to talk to ourselves like this. Used regularly, the mind's reflective influence can helpfully modify the impulsive brain. Thinking before acting can become a new habit. We are not after all puppets of our biological brain. We can be governors of our choices by using our constructed mind.

Four

How the 'Habit Brain' Learns

The Brain loves Repetition

I don't want you to think that the previous chapter implies that choosing is simple – especially when we are attempting to change something we repeatedly do. Although our conscious mind can modify the established pattern of our brain, it takes effort!

An important feature of our unconscious brain - all that furiously busy activity that never reaches our conscious mind - is that the connections it lays down between the neurons create pathways that are designed to be used repeatedly and often. Each human brain contains 86 million specialised nerve cells (neurons). Between the neurons there are many trillions of connections. I read recently that during the time it takes to say: 'synaptic connection', a million connections between neurons are made inside your brain!

Using this gigantic connecting machinery would be very hard work if we had to crank it into life to create every action: to make every cup of coffee; to choreograph every step when we walk, run or dance. Fortunately, once

The 'Habit Brain'

a sequence of synaptic connections is well-established, automation means that we can use it without conscious thought.

The more we use a sequence of behaviours, the more they become automatic. They act like an established groove in the sandy slope. This means that we don't have to re-create a behaviour every time we want one. When I say, "I would like tea, please", my host has a series of thoughts and actions pre-established and ready to go - initiating the behaviours needed to put a steaming cup in front of me. Just think how difficult it would be if this simple behaviour had to be created every time. Habits are our friends!

Silken Thread into Steel Cable

If we were able to look behind the curtain of consciousness, what we would find is that the brain establishes complex networks of connections between neurons to create a behaviour. The first time that behaviour is used, these connections and the order in which they are activated are quite tenuous, and we need a great deal of conscious support to activate them. I think of it as like creating a fragile filament of neural connections. However, every time we use the same strand - the same network of brain connections - the fragile thread is strengthened and becomes more substantial.

So, when a complex behaviour is repeated often enough it becomes supported by a powerful chain of connections. The single filament becomes an immensely complex sequence of automatic links. No conscious control is needed. What was once a tenuous filament is now a durable cable. Watch a young mother run after her wayward child. The toddler is swaying and jerking, struggling for coordination. The neural connections are under construction so there is a lot of hesitancy and correction in the awkward motion of the child. In contrast, the young mother streaks fluently across the grass in coordinated motion. Conscious control is not needed: she learned to run years ago. Now she naturally uses that automated behaviour.

We call this process of habituation through repeated practice **learning**. What we first practise under the strict gaze of our conscious awareness, later we can do automatically. Most learning is like this. At first, we are awkward; then proficient; then we reach a level where we execute the skill or use the knowledge without even being aware of what we are doing.

The Creation of Choice

Of course, this habituation can be a curse as well as a blessing! We are blessed with the ability to accumulate new behaviours and skills and automate their use for almost all of our lives. Without thinking, the athlete changes direction and clears an obstacle in a stride - even in a totally new situation. Practice has automated the extensive repertoire of behaviours that she or he needs to call on without conscious thought. However, this same habituation of behaviour can become an impediment whenever we try to change any well-learned practice or deeply-embedded thinking process.

For most of the first two decades of our life, our brain is a fertile field for new connections. After that, it gradually becomes less malleable, especially if new learning is neglected. As a result, when we grow past our teens, the capacity to learn new behaviours and replace old ones becomes more of an effort. Acquiring new behaviours becomes more difficult - but the capacity to learn never disappears!

We need our habits in order to become functional creatures, but they do make it more difficult to make different choices. It's easier to stay on the well-worn track of our habitual thoughts and actions than to blaze a new trail!

It is reassuring to know that what is involved in changing a habit is exactly what was involved in first acquiring one. Through the exercise of our will, the power of the mind to re-model the brain begins with the effortful creation of a new fragile thread of connections. This new tenuous pathway

The 'Habit Brain'

supports a new behaviour or a different way of thinking. With practice, requiring repetition and determination, this new filament of possibility is transformed into an alternative chain of connection. After a time[1] the new way of doing things becomes as viable as the old. We have a choice now: to use an old behaviour which does not serve us well, or to activate the new one which will enhance our power and freedom.

The Re-Construction of Self

This opportunity for new learning throws up a completely new dimension of the challenge to re-make our lives in order to optimise our personal freedom and individual satisfaction. As individuals, we construct ourselves: our identity, our values and beliefs, our capabilities, and skills from the moment when we begin to distinguish ourselves from our parents. In the early years of our lives, we are choosing blindly, taking the options that seem best in the moment. The problem is that we are undertaking a long-term project with short-term thinking. It's like beginning to build a house brick by brick, without any real sense of what the finished product will look like.

Inevitably, we will discover, as we mature through the mist of uncritical optimism into the brutal light of life's realities, that the house is not as good as it could be. If we could start again from scratch, we would perhaps not construct ourselves with the same behaviours and beliefs, the identical capabilities and customary preferences with which we now find ourselves.

---

[1] It takes a minimum of 21 days to habituate a new behaviour according to Maxwell Malt in 'Psycho-Cybernetics' 1989. Newer scientific studies have suggested that months may be needed before a complex new behaviour is fully habituated. On the other hand, instant learning is possible when the subsequent pain or pleasure is intense. Many of us 'learn' that we can't do something after a single painful failure.

Too often, we then conclude that 'I am what I am' and 'It's too late to change'. But from the perspective of mind and brain, it's never too late! Unless our brain is physically damaged, its ability to make new connections is with us until we die. The mind's influence can re-model the brain's activity as effectively when we are eighty as when we are eight – if we make the effort. As we grow older, the only impediment is that the effort required increases.

Which takes us back to the first line of this chapter: choice is always possible, but rarely straightforward. We can, and do, learn new behaviours, but naturally enough we usually only attempt that change when we can see that it would be worthwhile. There has to be a pay-off in terms of greater satisfaction or effectiveness for us to make the effort. We have to believe that new learning will close *the Gap*.

When learning a new behaviour does become more attractive, more likely to narrow *the Gap* than an old habit, we can - and do - choose to change.

Genetic Needs

Five

Our Genetic Needs

Genetic Instructions

Baby turtles struggle their way out of an egg buried in the sand, emerging at night into a hostile world. They have to know in which direction to scuttle if they are to get to the sea. Instinct tells them that there is danger - so they have to get there fast. Once in the sea, there is no protective parent waiting for them. They have to be able to feed themselves and look after themselves. How do they know so much when they have only just hatched?

Turtles are able to deal with these first difficult hours of their emergence in the world because they are born with a very precise set of genetic instructions. They are pre-programmed to do what is needed to survive. Humans, on the other hand, have no such detailed blueprint to follow. At our birth, we are helpless; unable to survive on our own. We remain relatively dependent for many years.

Unlike the turtle and other more primitive creatures, humankind is not born with a preponderance of imprinted behaviours. We are designed to learn - to gradually (and sometimes painfully) acquire the capabilities that we need to survive and thrive. We are constantly presented with choices about how to construct ourselves and how to make our way in the world.

However, we do have very powerful and enduring genetic prescriptions of our own. These enduring directives, our genetic **needs,** are far more flexible than the exact programs inherited by simpler creatures. Because our needs are not tied to specific behaviours, we have many ways to satisfy them. We don't choose our needs. We do choose how to gratify them.

Human Needs

We share with all creatures a need to survive – the universal directive that applies to all life forms. Apart from that, our other genetic commands are psychological: they enable us to build capabilities that surpass those of every other creature, and we continue to add to these capabilities throughout our lives – when we choose to.

There are several versions of this catalogue of genetic necessities. Psychiatrists William Glasser and Abraham Maslow, Researchers Edward Deci and Richard Ryan, Holocaust survivor Victor Frankl, and authors Martin Seligman and Daniel Pink each present their own variations. I will present what I believe can be described as the consensus between their views.

We all have genetic needs for:
Belonging (love, relatedness, connectedness, personal association).
Success (power, achievement, status, to feel in control).
Freedom (autonomy, self-determination, free will).
Survival (safety, certainty, nutrition, reproduction, rest).

It is worth mentioning that Glasser believed that **learning** itself is also a genetic need. While others regard learning as the genetic disposition that is central to our ability to survive, Glasser argued very persuasively that

Genetic Needs

the conjunction between learning and pleasure is significant. He put **fun and learning** together as a cognitive need.

Coming from a different perspective, Victor Frankl[1] believed that the impulse to discover **meaning**, a purpose for our lives, is also need-satisfying. Some believe that this may be just one of the dimensions of our need for power. However, in the search for life-satisfaction beyond survival, there are reasons to pay attention to Frankl's thesis. The search for meaning may not be as immediately compelling as the need to be powerful and free, but it seems that it may be strongly implicated in distinguishing between thriving and simply surviving.

As you can see, there are lots of similarities and a few differences between the ways in which the needs are identified. For us, how we name the needs is not as important as knowing that we have them. In turn, knowing that we have genetic needs is of less significance than how we choose to satisfy them.

Because gratifying or satisfying these needs is a source of pleasure, we are motivated to find ways of enhancing our well-being through the promise of these pleasurable feelings. From the moment of our birth, we discover ways to experience this pleasure and we are accomplished archivists of these experiences. When we have discovered that something is need-satisfying, we try to repeat or approximate it (or find an even better experience to replace it). Because we all find different ways in which to satisfy our needs, we discover personally specific experiences, people or events that elicit this pleasure. These personally need-satisfying (or 'quality') experiences provide reference points for us as we seek contentment and happiness. They provide 'the ideal' with which we compare 'the real'. They form the positive pole of *the Gap* that we are always attempting to narrow.

---

[1] Victor Frankl: 'Man's Search for Meaning', 1946.

Needs Conceive 'Wants'

Whatever the needs are named, these genetic drivers underpin the 'wants' that we experience. Our 'wants' are personal units of need-satisfaction: the quality moments, people and ideas that become the markers against which we compare our present perceptions. The pleasure that we feel from those experiences (the reason that we add particular 'wants' to our ideal world) arises from the satisfaction of one or several needs. Need-satisfaction is common to all. The way in which we satisfy the needs is individual.

Because they are commissioned by our genes (the biological fragments of human heredity) our needs cannot be ignored. When a need is being satisfied we don't notice it much and it plays little part in our day-to-day motivation. However, when a need is unsatisfied, *the Gap* between the real and the ideal becomes intrusive. The 'ideal' in our heads increasingly throws up 'wants' that are related to the need that is being denied.

This is easiest to notice when the survival need is concerned. When we feel hungry, our food-related 'wants' soon intrude into our thinking. Even if I am dieting (because my power need or relationship need have produced an ideal picture of a thinner me), the feelings of hunger initiated by my survival need are distressingly present.

In the same way, I may continue to turn up at my boring job and put up with my overbearing boss, but my need for autonomy and fun will become increasingly intrusive. The 'wants' associated with greater autonomy and more interesting work will present themselves to me constantly. It's these wants that I will compare to my present experience of work. When there is a *Gap*, the resulting frustration will keep intruding on my thoughts. However strong my yearning for certainty and financial survival may be, it will be hard to let go of my persistent urge to quit and look for a more satisfying job.

Genetic Needs

Learning Emancipates Us

The biological platform on which human development is built is our capacity for learning. We may be born without much in the way of capabilities, but we acquire them rapidly. The impulse to learn, and the way that the brain uses the pleasurable effects of dopamine to initiate learning and then reward it, is a masterpiece of biological design[2]. With this gene-supported capacity for adaptation, we not only develop new capabilities continually, but also learn in ways that enable us to become unique individuals. The creative capacity of the brain to suggest novel ways of responding to circumstances means that, as we learn, we individuate ourselves; we become different from other humans. My way of communicating my preferences, looking for love, expressing my thoughts, or relaxing when tired is different from yours. And between any two people there are many thousands of these differences.

This means that the needs are generic, but that the 'wants' are particular to every individual. Our 'wants' are the experiences and encounters in our lives that we come to believe will satisfy each of our needs. The prodigious variety of possible 'wants' is one of the two major sources of human difference - (the other is our varied perceptions of the world around us).

Many ways to Satisfy a Need

We can satisfy our need for **capability** (power or achievement) through skill acquisition, personal achievement, seeking status or superiority, feeling successful, showing competence, being in-control, or gaining recognition. Throughout our lives, we will seek the contentment of satisfying this need to feel powerful in these or other ways. When the need

---

[2] The neuro-transmitter Dopamine acts in two ways to support learning. The anticipation of learning generates an initial charge of this pleasure-inducing hormone to encourage effort. The sense of 'knowing' or achieving releases another injection of this natural 'feel-good' substance.

is unsatisfied, our sense of well-being diminishes. The less capable we feel the more our mind will be engaged in seeking ways to improve the situation.

As we evolve and come to understand ourselves, the ways in which we satisfy this need often change. As a skinny kid, I fed my power need by telling outrageous lies (it seemed to work at the time!). When I discovered I was a good runner, competitive success became my chief medium for the satisfaction of the need for power and achievement. However, being a competitor is not a good paradigm for a career of teaching or leadership. I came to realise that 'power-with' works better than 'power-over' in those roles. In the latest iteration of my attempts to feel powerful, I have become more focused on the ways in which I can **em**power other people. The need itself did not change – it could not. The ways I have chosen to satisfy the need has formed and transformed my life.

All our needs offer a variety of individual expression in this way. The need for autonomy might urge us to seek freedom from perceived constraints, or freedom to have multiple options; or might increase our hunger to be self-determined and independent from the control of others. Because of this need, we almost always want to behave willingly rather than from duty or imposition.

Our need for love and belonging provides the motivation to enter relationships; make friends; find a partner; belong to groups or teams; feel connected to our colleagues and friends and to be affiliated with like-minded people.

All the wants, the quality pictures that motivate us to behave, satisfy one or more of our needs. In this way, these deep genetic wellsprings of our development as individuals are the invisible but persistent drivers of the choices we make. In the process of choosing, we are always selecting options that seem likely to enhance our need-satisfaction in the ways that make sense to us.

Genetic Needs

The key difference between existing and flourishing may be the ways in which we choose to satisfy our needs. The hedonistic impulse directs us to the fastest route to need-satisfaction, the immediate sugar hit of the easily attainable. The long grind of working deliberately towards meaningful goals provides deeper satisfaction. It offers the sense that we are in control of *the Gap*, minding it deliberately.

It seems that the achievement of contentment requires not the simple satisfaction of our needs but something more ambitious: willingness to examine the ways in which we address our needs. Through reflective attention, sometimes called mindfulness, we can examine, develop and transform the way our needs are satisfied.[3]

Although we are all always striving to satisfy our needs, it is how we achieve that gratification that matters. There is evidence that our well-being depends on us finding ways to satisfy our needs that bring more than short-term bursts of pleasure.

Many Choices

In this diversity of need-satisfying options, we are very different from the turtle. Marine reptiles have few choices: their genetic blueprints are too prescriptive. For them, surviving and thriving depend on following the precise patterns with which they were equipped when they were hatched. In contrast, to be human is to be an inheritor of the freedom to make very personal choices from the immense smorgasbord of potentially need-satisfying experiences.

By design, we are creatures of choice.

---

[3] Stanley Cavell: 'Pursuits of Happiness', 1984.

Section 2: Managing the Gap

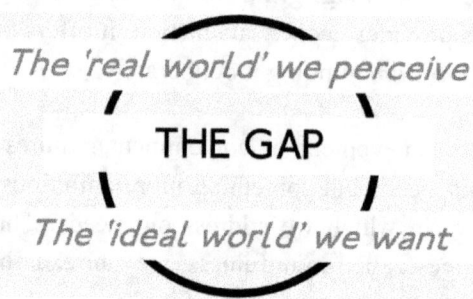

"The best years of your life are the ones in which you decide your problems are your own. You realize that you control your own destiny."

Albert Ellis

"Everything in your life is a reflection of a choice you have made. If you want a different result, make a different choice."

William Glasser

Six

A Pivotal Choice - To Be in Control

A Debilitating Fiction - Somebody made me do it!

The most important choice we make is the choice to see ourselves as in control of our own behaviours. It is a choice with enormous consequences. It will have a greater impact on our well-being and sense of freedom than any other choice we will make. When we know and appreciate that we can direct our own choices, we can manage our mind and choose actions to make life better. If we are not in control, we are indeed helpless.

Let me ask you this question:
"Do you prefer to be the person controlling your own life and to be responsible for your own well-being <u>or</u> would you rather allow your life to be controlled by other people and by circumstances?"

What did you answer?

Most people respond by saying that they would greatly prefer to be in control. Indeed, people are often puzzled about why I even bother to ask the question.

I ask the question because it's all too easy to assert that our personal freedom is important to us, and then to heedlessly give it away. Of course, we rarely choose to deliberately relinquish our autonomy, but it is tempting to become seduced by the language and opinions around us. We are immersed in the parlance of social communication that is saturated with the presupposition that we are controlled by other people and events. All around us we hear expressions that inaccurately connect what we are experiencing **internally** with information and events which are **outside** us.

Although they sound similar, there is a world of difference between the thoughts expressed by these two pairs of sentences:
1. *"I decided to have nothing more to do with him."*
2. *"I had no choice - I had to end our relationship."*

And similarly:
1. *"As circumstances changed, I decided to change my plans."*
2. *"His interference and bad manners made me change my plans."*

They don't sound much different from each other, but they are contrasting in their meaning. In each pair of sentences the circumstances are the same. In the first pair, I perceived a reason for terminating a friendship. In the second pair, I opted to alter my future plans. What is different is the way I attribute responsibility. In the first sentence of each pair, I am taking responsibility for my feelings and actions. In the second, I am not. It is through the pre-suppositions embedded in this second formulation that we too easily surrender to the idea that circumstances control us.

The Erroneous Assumptions of External Control

The second statement of each pair of statements shares two common assumptions:
1. That something outside me can 'cause' me to do or think things.
2. That the external event justifies or excuses the action I took.

Being in Control

These pre-suppositions are not only invalid but also potentially harmful. If they become my habitual thinking, the way I talk to myself about people and events, they constitute a surrender of my free will - a capitulation to the tide of events that flows around me. If I speak and think like this, I am surrendering the steering wheel of my life by telling myself that I have no other options.

Let's review from the first few chapters what we already know about the human control system. We know that we receive information through our senses and then make sense of that information in order to act on it. All of the information begins outside us. As soon as it moves inside our container of skin, the information is interpreted within the organism we call 'self'. All of the processing between the sensory receipt of the information and the behaviour we choose happens inside us. That process is an inside job!

Where Choice Happens

I am not challenging the 'facts' - the information that is 'out there'. I am not denying that at times any of us may feel offended, coerced, or manipulated into a situation where succumbing to circumstances or the will of others seems to be our best option. We all do encounter information from our senses, and subsequently decide to act upon it. We become aware of behaviour we do not like; many of us hear negative opinions about other people; sometimes individuals act in ways that we resent; other individuals behave in ways that we experience as painful and distressing. And within ourselves most of us experience emotions so strong that they feel compelling.

In actuality, however, the events and actions of other people do not 'make' us do anything. Unless they are compelling us by overwhelming physical force, all another person's behaviour can give us is information. Linking antecedent occurrences outside our own organism with our own subsequent action does not prove causality. We always have a choice about how to respond to circumstances or to other people's behaviour.

The assumption that there is a *causal* connection between events in the world **outside** ourselves and the behaviours that we generate from **inside** our own mind is always invalid. Whenever we speak, think, or act as if something outside ourselves compelled our internal decision-making, we are undermining our own free will and our ability to self-determine our behaviours.

The Pain we Avoid

I have written elsewhere about an early encounter with attempts by my teachers to control me. It was such an important experience for me because it has helped me to understand how important our internal choices always are, even in the face of painful external events.

Like many boys of my generation (and some girls too) I was physically hurt by my teachers to encourage me to learn. Such was the ignorance about human motivation at that time, they were probably thinking that this would actually help me. Long before psychological research helped us to understand the mechanism of choice, humans knew that our control system is designed to avoid pain as well as to prefer pleasure. As a result, my teachers, like many adults of generations past, systematically used pain to 'encourage' me. When I did not learn my Latin vocabulary to the standard required, I was caned - beaten across the bottom, legs or on the hand with a bamboo stick.

I quite often encounter men of my age who claim that they were taught to behave respectfully, study hard and 'become the man I am today' as a result of their capitulation to the teachers who caned them. I am sure there were many young people who decided that behaving well and studying hard was preferable to being repeatedly hit. I was not one of them!

My experience was different. My resentment at this deliberate (and to my mind outrageously unfair) caning was to choose resistance. I refused to be bullied into compliance. I resented the teachers involved so vehemently

Being in Control

that I decided to show them that they could never thrash me into submission. I steadfastly refused to yield to the tyrants who were attempting to intimidate me into compliance. I decided that I would not ever learn my Latin homework. I did not!

With the benefit of hindsight, I now understand my eleven-year-old self. I chose the external pain of regular beating over the internal pain of giving in. The pleasure of exerting my free will, the feeling of personal power that accompanied my defiance, was internal and telling. I knew from that day that I was internally controlled, a child of choice.[1]

Internal Control

Remember that in earlier chapters I described the way in which every one of us is designed as an internal control system. We compare what we want with what is happening; then if there is a separation between the two, we select a behaviour to narrow *the Gap*. That's something that happens inside us: a thought or decision generated inside our own mind. That is how the mind initiates a behaviour. If you inflict physical hurt on me, I can choose how to respond. If you say something that I interpret as mean, or you act in a manner that I consider unfair - and I become angry and lash out at you - then that is an action that I take. You did not and could not 'make' me do it!

The choice to live congruently with this reality is the greatest step we can take to ensure our own personal freedom – our liberty to choose. When we take ownership of our own behaviour, we are assuming control of our life and circumstances. When we choose to think and behave as if other

---

[1] Of course, as with all behaviours, there were consequences. I denied myself an understanding of language and its origins which would have been useful to me as an adult. With foresight I might have chosen differently - but we make many of our choices without the benefit of prescience!

people are controlling us, we hand over the management of our lives and our happiness to them.

Scientifically, the evidence is conclusive. Other people and events are not inside the control system we call 'self'; not inside our 'bag of skin'. We are all controlled from the inside. Whatever is happening outside us (and there is often a great deal going on in the world around us) we are in control of how to respond. Making *the choice* to accept this reality is the first and most important decision we can make to ensure our individuality and freedom. Making this choice opens up the whole world of self-determination. It allows us to take charge of the present moment and to be architects of our own future

Circumstances affect our Choices

I am not distorting or being fanciful about reality as I write this. The circumstances of life are often unfair; we may be bullied or criticised; terrible events may buffet our composure; other people may hurt us deliberately, either through action or neglect. All these things happen. We often have no control over these events outside ourselves. Tragedy and pain intrude on the serenity of all of us at some point in our life. Life is difficult![2]

We often point to the comparative helplessness of children when we think about the limits of our choices. There is a huge power differential between children and adults that only resolves itself as the children mature into adulthood. Many children have few choices, most notably in situations where they are tightly controlled or treated abusively by adults.

All that is true. An important part of the explanation offered in his book is that we have limited influence over events <u>outside</u> our own body.

---

[2] These first words of Scott Peck's influential book ' The Road Less Travelled' had a strong influence on my thinking. As he mentions, they mirror the first of the Buddha's Four Noble Truths: ' Life is Suffering'.

Being in Control

Nonetheless, we are still in control of the choices of the one person we can control - ourselves. Each of us can choose how to respond to troubling people or events. We can always choose - even if some circumstances leave us with very few palatable choices. Even children, whose few accessible choices may bring the risk of pain or rejection, have some options in the face of the disproportionate power of the adults in their lives.

The Last of the Human Freedoms

Victor Frankl, surviving in cruelly inhumane conditions in a Nazi Concentration Camp, wrote: *"Everything can be taken from a man but ...the last of the human freedoms - to choose one's attitude in any given set of circumstances, to choose one's own way."*[3]

Whatever the events in our external world, and whatever the limitations those events impose on us, there is as space between those events and the response we create internally – in our own mind. In that space, in the choices we make about how to respond, are autonomy, power and freedom.

I agree that's not what we hear from many others. Daily we hear from the media, our neighbours and even our leaders that we are made victims by the actions or oppression of others; by the economic circumstances of our lives; by our personal or racial history; or by the mischief of our critics. These things may happen, but they can't cause our behaviour or dictate our response; and they can't make us victims unless we choose to act as though we are helpless.

---

[3] Victor Frankl, a World War 2 Concentration Camp survivor who documented his experiences (and his conclusions about those experiences) in his book 'Man's Search for Meaning', 1946.

The great endowment of human freedom comes with a caveat: we are responsible for what we do - for how we respond to the shadows and sunbeams of life.

When we have made that one pivotal choice in our life: that we are always self-determined and always responsible for our own choices, then we have taken a giant step towards personal independence. We have chosen to steer our own course; to stamp our lives with 'Created by ME'!

Making this choice opens up the avenues of opportunity. If **I** am responsible for my life, then I can manage it. I can make changes to my behaviour and to my responses. If I am prepared to make the effort, I can learn how to manage my emotions. I can learn to adjust my actions so that I behave in ways that attract friends and influence those around me.

This choice to be self-determined comes with one troubling implication: if other people can't control me, I can't control them either!

Seven

Choosing to Give Up Control

Abandoning the Enticing Illusion of Control!

There is one challenging inference that flows from knowing and accepting that the only person I can control is myself:

I can't control other people!

Accepting this - and behaving in a way that is congruent with this unsettling truth - may be the second most important choice we make in the pursuit of our own sense of well-being.

We can enhance our understanding of the mind and apply this knowledge to managing ourselves and developing our own capabilities. If we do this, our **self-control** will improve.

It's easy to imagine that this mechanism of self-control applies to our management of other people. It does not! What happens inside ourselves is not a metaphor for what happens outside! We can't manage other people by our own act of will. None of the tools of self-management will help us to establish control over other people.

Every person is his or her own control system. Every individual is designed to pursue their own path to self-management and contentment. And much as we are often seduced by the belief that we know what is best for other people, acting upon that belief reduces our influence and damages relationships.

Because what other people do matters to us, it often seems unfortunate that we have to rely upon their cooperation - but can't command it. It would be so much easier if we could insist that they follow our plans and prescriptions for them!

Life would be so much simpler for us as parents and partners, teachers, leaders, managers or politicians if we could just speak and 'the other' would follow our lead. Taking the time to influence the thinking and behaviour of another independent control system is such hard work! It depends on us being so persuasive or personally credible that the other person agrees willingly to adopt our ideas and goals as their own.

Once again, it comes back to the design of the human control system. Our neural networks are designed for internal control. The brain has no mechanisms for directly interfering with the neurology of another human being.[1] When we attempt to step beyond the boundaries of our own control, we are inviting resistance from the gene-created autonomy of another organism. When what we want is the cooperation of another person, another control system, we can only succeed when they decide to want what **we** want. Respecting the free will and personal autonomy of other people is the hallmark of the difference between legitimate influence and coercion.

---

[1] This is not to say that we are incapable of influence. We can all learn to use language and behaviours that will encourage other people to choose what we want them to choose. We can sway people, but we can't compel them.

Giving up Control

The Coercion Trap

When we attempt to push others towards compliance, to exert our own will - when we *insist* - then we experience the *push-back* which is the automatic response of another individual to attempted control. It's a genetic brain response - a built-in protection.

Despite this, many of us find it difficult to give up the habit of attempting to control. To some extent this is understandable. Because we are always trying to close the divide between what **we** want and whatever **we** perceive, it's natural to try to change the behaviour of others when their thoughts and actions seem to be creating *the Gap* that we are experiencing.

A significant result of behaving as though other people can be made to do things is that it feeds back into our own pre-suppositions. The cycle of external control has its own misleading logic: if **I** can control someone, this means that other people are able to control me. These assumptions lead us in two opposing but equally unhelpful directions: one the one hand, to the surrender of our own responsibility; on the other hand, to trespassing on the intrinsic freedom of others.

Unhappily, it's this second inclination that can be the most harmful. We may experience our children's behaviour, the volatility of our boss, or the noise from the neighbours across the street as a trigger for frustration - so we try to craft a behaviour that we hope will change them. In the face of the unwanted circumstances that result from other people's behaviour, we feel relatively helpless, so we try to re-establish control of our lives by imposing our will on other people.

However, trying to control the world around us as if it were the same as the world inside our own minds is not liberating. Its effects are actually the opposite: they take us more deeply into personal enslavement.

Enslaving Ourselves

When we are focused on trying to change other people; when we think our own satisfaction depends upon our success in managing the behaviour of someone else, we are no longer behaving freely and pursuing our own well-being – we have given that away in exchange for trying to limit the freedom and autonomy of others.

The frustration of attempting to change a situation that is out of our control can easily become compulsive. *The Gap* on which we are focused can become our obsession. We are held captive by the effect that we are trying to achieve.

Unsuccessful attempts to control other people imprison us as nothing else can. We fall into the tyrant trap! It's a three-step process:
> 1. We decide that we know what is right because it feels right for us.
> 2. We conclude that what is right for us should be right for everyone.
> 3. Once we have worked out what is right for other people, we easily draw the conclusion that we have a duty to impose our version of 'right' on someone else - to try to control their behaviour!

The consequence of that spiral into tyranny is that we surrender to the control of other people's apparent intransigence. Even when our coercion is successful (and it rarely will be!) our life becomes distorted by trying harder and harder to force other people to do what we want. This preoccupation does nothing to support our own well-being. The people we are trying to control are unwittingly controlling us through their non-compliance.

Whenever I am trapped in the cycle of trying to impose my control over another independent organism, I am introducing distress into both of our lives. I will be frustrated and angry because someone won't do what I want them to do. They will be distressed and unhappy because I am trying to force them to do something they don't want to do.

Giving up Control

As a school Principal, I spent a great deal of time in conversation with the unhappy parents of unhappy teenagers. Young people of that age are genetically pre-disposed to begin the changes that will allow them to become independent of their parents. Parents are often unwilling to relinquish that dependence. The result is that intra-family battles are constantly simmering about such things as tidiness, study habits, the influence of friends, 'attitude', parties, planning or future goals. The more the parents attempt to coerce, the more resistance they experience.

The question is: 'Are the parents experiencing their own freedom and well-being in their attempts to impose their will on their children?' No, they are not! Because the parents are sure that they are right, they intensify their attempts to control, and in doing so sacrifice their own present sense of contentment and also risk their future relationship with their child - all in the false hope that they will be able to regain control.

Parenting

I am certainly not implying that parents should not care about the welfare of their teenage children. Managing the transition to adulthood with love and understanding is one of the most demanding tasks faced by every parent. However, it's really helpful for parents when they understand the nature of this transition. As creatures with their own needs to satisfy, maturing children are bound to move towards independence. The long years of reliance that are a defining characteristic of human development can't last for ever. Our children would never be liberated to lead their own lives if they were tied to our nurturing guidance for ever. The loving control that was responsible parenting through infancy and childhood must give way to separateness and mutual respect, in order for the cycle of generation to be completed.

The challenges of this common experience are faced most effectively by parents who make the choice to manage the only person whom they can actually control – themselves! Choosing to be responsible for their own behaviours as parents and focusing on the contribution that they can make to the relationship with their 'difficult' teenager, is both an act of personal freedom and a demonstration of it. The mum or dad who makes it clear to their child that they are loved unconditionally; that they are committed to do whatever they can to remain connected; that they will listen with understanding to the perception of the young person, is exercising and showing respect for personal freedom.

We want our children to know that they have choices at this time in their lives; to be able to talk openly about the consequences of these choices so that we they will become skilled at managing their own freedom and take responsibility for making good choices.

The choice to parent in this way - by keeping the relationship (and therefore the influence) strong - is critical. If we choose the 'attempting to control' route, the relationship will be easily damaged. Paradoxically, in trying to impose change on a child, we diminish the natural influence we have.

It is easy to be seduced by the 'tough-talking' parenting that sounds good to the unreflective ear but does harm in practice. The 'my way or the highway' kind of ultimatum that desperate parents often contemplated in their conversations with me may appear to be strong but is actually just a 'dummy-spit' by them! That approach postures as if it's tough, but it's actually an easy surrender.

Real tough love is responsible parenting: parenting that understands that managing our choices as parents is the most powerful illustration for our teens of how to manage theirs. It's really challenging to advise but not coerce; to remain open and listening despite the trepidation we feel; to concede the inevitability of the experimentation of youth while urging them to be cautious, to stay safe. Like every challenge in life, the choice to be in control of everything that we **can** control - by choosing total responsibility for our own behaviours - is demonstrated by this example.

Whether we are parenting, teaching, leading, managing, or being a friend, the twin dynamics of keeping the relationship strong while respecting the

Giving up Control

autonomy of the other apply. These behaviours improve the relationship. The better the relationship, the stronger the influence. As my colleague Judy Hatswell is wont to say: "We have to give up control to gain control."

Through the processes of our mind we can control our responses - our thoughts and behaviour - through every unpredictable or daunting challenge. It's the powerful choice we need to make to prepare ourselves for the other choices that will promote and enhance our personal freedom - not only the decision to relinquish our attempts to control others, but also the resolve to be resilient, emotionally mature, and confident in the face of the choices of others.

The choice is stark: if my well-being is entangled in your compliance, I am a prisoner of my unavailing attempts to change you.

I am liberated only if I recognise and accept that, like me, you are making choices. Knowing that I can responsibly do my best to be persuasive but remain respectful and supportive in the face of our differences, I can allow myself to be both powerful and free.

MINDING THE GAP

Eight

The Limits of Choice

What We Can Choose and What We Can't

In an era when many of the gurus of self-help seem to be proclaiming that we can do anything we choose - or be whoever we want to be - I am offering a more sober and pragmatic prediction.

> We always have choices.
> Our choices **are** more numerous than we sometimes assume.
> Our choices are **not** unlimited.

As a young athlete I wanted to be able to run fast – to be a sprinter. I trained and trained. I spent my small savings on weight-training equipment and starting blocks. I ran up hills for power and down hills for speed. Nothing I tried made a significant difference to how fast I ran. To be able to run lightning fast (as I now know) a person needs a preponderance of 'fast-twitch' fibres in their muscles. If you don't have them, you can't grow them. I could improve my speed to some extent, but I was never going to be a successful sprinter. However, I did realise - as a result of all my running - that I could keep training for long periods. I had

Choices have Limits

the high levels of endurance that result from a robust cardio-vascular system and a preponderance of 'slow-twitch' muscle fibres. I made a sensible choice: I chose to be a long-distance runner. It was not my first choice, but it was a choice.

The distinction between: 'We always have choices' and 'We can do whatever we choose' is significant. Our choices are never unlimited: they have boundaries. I can choose to order tea or coffee in my favourite café, but as they don't sell alcohol, choosing a malt whisky is not possible; it's not available. I may want my children to become responsible and contented without them having to learn from painful experience, but I don't have a magic wand. There is no shortcut to learning.

Choices have Limits

Like the limitations imposed by my muscle fibres, or the menu in my café, our options are bounded by what's available to us: in some circumstances by our particular combination of biological assets; sometimes by the landscape of our environment; at times by our history and opportunities.

There is a fine line here. Although some things are unattainable because of personal limits or circumstances, these are far fewer than we usually imagine. We are more likely to be restricted by artificial limits that we impose upon ourselves than by any real boundary of ability or physiology.

Both Sides of the Curtain of Consciousness

This is where understanding the nature of brain as well as mind is so helpful in managing our mental processing. Behind the curtain of the unconscious, the brain either has a schema (an existing network of nerve cell connections) for a behaviour or capability, or it doesn't. If it does not have a schema, then at that moment we literally 'can't do' that behaviour. It follows that in front of the curtain our conscious representation of the absence of an enabling schema is 'I can't do that' – but this does not necessarily mean I can't **ever** do that – just that I can't do it **yet**! The learning and practice needed to form the relevant congregation of neural connections have not yet happened.

Now, if we switch our focus to the mind - the conscious mode which is in front of our curtain of awareness - there is a real contradiction. The mind tends to take the point-in-time actuality of 'not having learned something yet' and generalise it to create a timeless truth: 'I can't do that.' This is a weird kind of 'one-step learning'; it's very common but it's rarely helpful.

The 'I can't' experience is why the mind often only needs to be conscious of just one 'failure' to conclude that some behaviour or achievement is beyond our reach. When our children succumb to this generalisation and say that they 'can't do' something, we wisely recognise the fallacy. We help them through the learning stages and encourage them to keep practising. Sadly, when we become older - when we have reached a point in our lives when the greater percentage of our behaviours has become habituated - we are often not so wise.

We Know our Limits by Testing Them

Here then is the paradox of choice. We can't choose anything (or everything) we want. Some things truly are beyond us. Conversely, we can choose most things we want if we dare, persist, and learn.

Only by testing our limits can we possibly resolve the paradox.

Whether we can or we can't, will only truly be discovered in the retrospective light of determined effort and relentless willingness to practise. In the absence of our willingness to commit in this way, the old adage will turn out to be true: 'Whether we think we can or think we can't, we're right!'

Choices have Limits

Deciding which Choices have the Most Value

Faced with many choices as we negotiate the pathways and junctions of life, it's helpful to remember a few simple principles:

1. We can accomplish many things that we aspire to; it is rare for a person to achieve everything that they aim for.
2. We can't choose backwards! Whether our past choices helped us or hurt us, we can't change them – but we can learn from them.
3. All choices that take us forward come with a price tag in terms of the time, effort and commitment required. Making the choices about which turnings to take, which tracks to follow and which capabilities to build is the key to making those commitments effectively.
4. Some choices are more important than others. Learning how to tell the difference is important.

Choosing is a Now and Future Activity

One of the ways in which we can waste many precious hours of life is wishing that we had made different choices in the past.

"If only......." we perseverate.
"If only I had chosen a different career."
"If only I had learned different skills."
"If only I had not been so stubborn."
"If only ...."
We can fill in the blanks for ourselves!

Expending energy on re-visiting past choices is simply spinning the wheels of our potential to be well and contented. "If only ...." defines our unhappiness and renders us powerless. We are not time-travellers. The human organism does not have a re-wind button. We can make choices now and for the future. We can never choose a different past!

Rather than spend time on what we can't change (mired in the helplessness of obsessing about the impossible) we can become powerful by designing the future. What's past is past and immutable. What **will be** is replete with possibility.

Adopting the A.C.T.[1] procedure takes us decisively forward:

Accept the situation. Whatever happens, or whatever anyone has done, there is little point in blaming, complaining, or making excuses. None of us has a magic wand that enables us to go back into the past and make changes. What is done is done. Accepting the situation liberates us to move on quickly.

Consider the CHOICES you have. However profound the problem, there are always choices. Our self-efficacy is eloquently demonstrated when we focus on 'What next?'. As Victor Frankl observed: "Life ultimately means taking the responsibility to find the answer to the problems it presents."

Take Action. Decisions are only really made when we act. It's important to move into the solution space by taking action as soon as possible. Almost all difficulties are exacerbated by inaction. 'Let's move on and improve' is the way to recover. Take action - even if the solution is imperfect.

I am not suggesting that acceptance is easy. When we seem consumed by regret or encumbered by memories of historical trauma, letting go of the past and turning our focus to the future may be one of the hardest things we have to do for ourselves. However, without taking this step we can very easily be drawn relentlessly backwards into a state of ill-being.

A.C.T is liberating: an investment in the future that frees us from the anchors of the past. It's something we can choose; an option that is always open to us.

---

[1] This is my version of the A.C.T. model which I learned from Dr. Ali Sahebi via Judy Hatswell who added a further letter to the acronym (S: self-evaluate) to make it A.C.T.S.

Choices have Limits

Whether the choices we make today will be decisive in securing our happiness and success is unknown and unknowable. Accepting the uncertainty of the world is one of the primary applications of A.C.T.

We will only know what is possible and productive by taking action, by testing our limits, by choosing the pathways that are most likely to help us thrive – not simply survive.

Nine

'Wants': Our Internal Reference Points

Choosing What We Really Want

Our reference points for 'the ideal' are our 'wants': the events, people, ideas or events that gratify one or more of our needs. Most of us can identify many things that we want. They may be experiences, activities, ideas or people. We believe that if we attain or encounter these desirable examples of the ideal, the quality of our lives will be improved.

Our wants may be attractive to us, but most of us have noticed that not all of them are good for us! Our store of ideal word pictures usually includes a good proportion of the 'need-satisfying but trivial' and often the 'need-satisfying but harmful' – not to mention the 'need-satisfying but unethical'! The brain can be very impulsive, and not always rational. It does not have a built-in moral compass. It needs the help of consciousness to work out what is best for us in the long term, and to grapple with 'right' and 'wrong'.

Our Internal Reference Points

Big questions that we must address in seeking our own well-being include: "How do I select the particular 'want' to focus on at any moment?"; "What do I really want?"; "What will serve me best in the long term?".

We can also help ourselves to experience well-being rather than frustration by pursuing rational and attainable wants. Spending our lives pursuing irrational[1] wants, or goals that are beyond our present reach, can impair us. Habituating the experience of failing to achieve what we want is not a recipe for well-being!

For most people, the massive storage facility of our brain accumulates many 'wants'; many examples of the memories and aspirations that hold the promise of closing *the Gap* between our perceptions and our ideal world. Unfortunately, storage capacity is not accompanied by limitless processing power. Our minds have a broad range but a narrow focus. We can't attend to all our 'wants' at the same time – in fact we can usually only pay attention to them one-by-one.

Across the globe there are many people with few, though unremitting, 'wants'. Living in poverty pares a person's quality world back to essentials, to the spare economy of daily survival. In contrast, in more affluent communities immersed in a world of commodities, the 'wants' can be innumerable. Many reliable studies show that monetary wealth is not necessarily accompanied by contentment. When there are few limits on the commodities available, hedonic adaptation soon erodes the pleasure of the experience. As Rousseau[2] put it: "These conveniences, by becoming habitual, entirely cease to be enjoyable." Even more telling, the resulting 'ennui' tends to exacerbate the sense of dissatisfaction.

---

[1] Albert Ellis drew attention to many irrational beliefs such as 'wanting to be loved and approved of by everyone', 'always being successful' and 'dependence on other people for happiness'. Ellis developed a Cognitive Therapy, Rational-Emotive Behaviour Therapy, based on the idea that irrational wants and self-defeating self-talk are a common basis of unhappiness.
[2] Jean-Jacques Rousseau: 'Discourse on Inequality' 1754.

If we come to believe that happiness can be achieved from the outside, by the accumulation of 'stuff' or the collection of the markers of external success, then we easily exhaust our happiness on the hedonic treadmill. As one box is ticked, the next one appears. It's in this way that people seek promotion to jobs for which they are unsuited, relentless expansion of their business, or 'the next level' in some sporting or social achievement. What Rousseau understood, and what our reflective mind can see (when we let it), is that moving on and up is progress without a destination. Just because it's the next step, the next revolution of the treadmill, does not equate with either progress or contentment. The hierarchies of our 'wanting' do not equate with levels of well-being.

Whatever our status or wealth, it's comparatively rare to sort our wants into any kind of priority. With so many possible 'wants' this can easily lead to a bit of a muddle – to paying only scant attention to what is really important, while yearning for the transient or trivial as they flutter through consciousness.

From Many 'Wants', which to Choose?

We think that we want many things. We have countless experiences, ideas, people, and events in our ideal world. An interesting exercise that you might like to try is to seat yourself in front of a blank page or screen and list all the things that you want. Ask yourself the question: "If I could have anything I want, so long as I write it on this page, what are the 'wants' I would be sure to write down?".

When I did this exercise, I stopped at about twenty because I only focused on some big 'wants'. Some people identify many more than that – especially if they note down all the details of their 'wants' such as every kitchen appliance they think will be useful, every city they want to visit, how they should be spoken to by other people, how a word should be pronounced, or the exact weather that's ideal for a walk along a beach.

Our Internal Reference Points

However many wants we have, we can focus on very few at any time, therefore our discontent is contained. Think of the inner turmoil it would create if we were comparing our present circumstances with every single picture of the 'ideal' at any one time. What a recipe for perennial frustration! Because of the many *'Gaps'* that would inevitably assail our consciousness, we would feel permanently dissatisfied.[3]

Remember that almost all the wants on our lists are either attempts to repeat, approximate, or improve experiences that we associate with pleasure. We often also include eventualities that we believe will bring future pleasure – like winning the lottery or getting a new job. Even those of us who have never experienced winning a great deal of money tend to imagine that it will satisfy many of the 'wants' in our ideal world. Although the research tells us that this is actually questionable - that winning money rarely enhances our well-being - the fancy that it does sells lottery tickets worth trillions of dollars each year!

These 'wants' make up one side of *the Gap* that we are always trying to close. On the other side of the divide are our perceptions of what is happening within us and around us. Our urge to close *the Gap* is what we usually describe as motivation. It is our frustration with a life that is not ideal that provides the energy for behaviour.

It doesn't matter if the person trying to close *the Gap* is an athlete training and striving to win a race or the game; a child throwing a tantrum over a toy or lolly denied them; a couple working through the obstacles to creating and sustaining a loving relationship; or a business professional trying to create a successful and profitable enterprise. In every situation, there is always that separation between what we want and the present situation to move us onward.

---

[3] Personalities who are very focused on the details of their personal preferences can easily become chronically unhappy because there are always aspects of their lived experience which are incompatible with one or more of their wants. Moments of pleasure are soon undermined by their recognition of another 'Gap'. Everyone's experience includes far more imperfection than instances of 'exactly right', so there will always be a 'Gap' to notice.

Which leads us back to choosing the particular want that we are focusing on at any one time.

Having so many 'wants', which ones do we weigh against our present perceptions? As I sit writing this page in Café Kirra[4] (my favourite coffee shop) I could pay attention to any of the 'wants-related' features that are immediate to my circumstances:
- The taste of my coffee.
- The comfort of my chair.
- The quality of the view.
- The paragraphs I have just written.
- My 'ideal' of myself as a competent author.

However, I can't keep even those five 'wants' in mind at once. If I am focused on my writing, I am not aware of the hardness of the chair. I often let my coffee go cold while I am trying to find the right phrase to express a thought.

How will your Life Change if you Get what you Want?

This ability to choose and focus on the wants that are most important to us contributes to our capacity to lead a satisfying life. If I spend time enjoying the taste of the coffee, or gazing glumly at the view and wishing that I was in France, time will pass - but I will leave the café feeling frustrated because I have made no progress towards my ideal of a completed book. I choose instead to concentrate my attention on writing cogently in order to communicate my beliefs about the cumulative importance of even trivial-seeming choices that have significance for tomorrow. Most lives are assembled like this - through the crumbs of

---

[4] A great deal of this book was written with a coffee at my elbow. My thanks to Dean and Lisa and the crew at Café Kirra for great coffee and a wonderful place to write.

Our Internal Reference Points

small options taken purposefully, rather than through rumination about grand decisions.

What this shows is that choosing the most helpful 'want' to pay attention to is one of the key choices presented to our awareness. And because the brain does not naturally put a priority on the 'wants', we have to establish relative importance through conscious consideration.

This is where the question: "How will my life change if I get what I want?" helps us. Knowing that our 'wants' present themselves to us in a constant stream of momentary glimpses of preference helps us to look out for those that are most important. Our fleeting desires flit across the landscape of our attention without a priority tag. There is often no indicator that 'this choice' will be significant in constructing the future and other choices will not. We must decide that for ourselves.

"How will achieving this 'want' change my life?" is a question that invites us to put a priority on our 'wants'. There's a subtle hierarchy among the images and experiences in our ideal world. Some events and experiences bring fleeting moments of satisfaction. When the coffee is gone, it's gone! Others provide for longer term need-satisfaction such as acquiring skills or capabilities that will enable us to repeat or intensify our feeling of competence and power.

We can apply a hierarchy suggested by Robert Dilts in his writing about logical levels.[5] Liberally interpreted, it might suggest that there is a hierarchy among our choices:

---

[5] Robert Dilts adapted ideas from Gregory Bateson and Bertrand Russell to describe the 'logical levels' of learning and change. Each level encompasses and organises the level below. Because these seem to correspond to levels of complexity in the brain, they are sometimes referred to as 'neurological' levels. http://www.nlpu.com/Articles/LevelsSummary.htm

> choosing how to see ourselves
> making choices about what to value
> choosing our goals and how to achieve them
> making choices that enable us to build our capabilities
> choosing behaviours that will satisfy our immediate needs

The choices made at the top level of the hierarchy almost always have implications for the choices below. Choices at the bottom of the pyramid don't necessarily make any difference to what is above.

Choosing how we want to see ourselves (our identity) and the values that will help us live as the person we want to be, guides us towards the goals that mark our journey. Being mindful of our core values directs us towards the acquisition of the capabilities we would like to develop. We choose behaviours that are goal-directed and valuable to us.

In contrast, choosing behaviours to satisfy an immediate need without reference to a goal-enabling capability leads us towards an accidental life – a mode of living and being that reacts to the immediate prompting of our hasty brain, not to the planned orchestration of our slower mind.

This hierarchy helps us to design ourselves from the top down – from who we would like to be, rather than simply what we want to do in the impulse of the moment. Starting from our sense of the person we would like to be enables us to design the future we want, decide on goals that will take us there, build the capabilities that we need to achieve our goals and then behave in ways that will develop those capabilities. There is a lot of merit in the wise advice to first write our own epitaph and then map our lives according to what we would like to see written.

The alternative is a kind of random life where we make a cascading series of short-term decisions – choices that bring immediate need-satisfaction but which may have little consequence for the future, or those that can leave us worse off. Not everything that is need-satisfying in the present

Our Internal Reference Points

moment can usher us towards a satisfying life. What feels good may not be good for us!

Attaining our well-being is inevitably a long-term project assembled across the stepping-stones of the choices we make day-by-day. That's the challenging reality. The source of optimism is the realisation that, whatever our present circumstances, we can always start again, working from the top of the hierarchy so that our future choices have a cumulative impact on our wellness and contentment.

Wishing and Wanting

Wishing, as I explain it, is the category of experiences that we think we would enjoy if they were to happen, but to which we are likely to commit little or no energy or effort. We tend to regards wishes as dependent on factors outside our control. Wishing is passive.

I think of wishes as coins dropped into the well of possibility; our expectations of the genie as we rub our lamp of optimism. Wishes are the stuff of reverie – the kind of daydreams that divert us from action.

It's natural to wish, but we rarely invest significant effort in our wishes. They are eventualities that would be nice if they were to happen to come along, but we rarely go out of our way to track them down. Wishes, like wants, may exist as pictures or ideas in our ideal world, but they either don't seem attainable by our own efforts or are too vague to generate action. Wishes hold us hostage to events that we can't control; captives to the lottery of life instead of governors of our future.

Only if we are actively pursuing a wish does it becomes a 'want'.

Think about the difference between 'wish' and 'want' in the way the mind works. If it's a 'want', then we will generate a behaviour to try to close *the Gap* between what we perceive and the 'want' we are pursuing. Our wants are both 'ideal and attainable' in our album of quality experience. Having a want urges us to do something to make that ideal happen. Wants are labelled with a price that we are willing to pay. We put effort into attaining our wants!

Wishes are not so motivating. They often don't pre-dispose us for action. If I **wish** to be rich, I might buy lottery tickets or fritter away my meagre savings in front of a poker machine, or perseverate about the unfairness of life. If I **want** to be rich, I will probably choose work options, business enterprises, entrepreneurial opportunities, and investments to earn whatever I conceive to be 'enough'. I will do real work to close *the Gap*.

It's important to notice that both a wish and a want expose us to the experience of *the Gap*. Both will produce frustration when there is a space between the ideal and the real. However, because the want can be actively pursued, the behaviours we generate in striving to close *the Gap* quieten our frustration. When we are behaving in a way in order to improve things, we are in the process of moving towards change that will begin to close *the Gap*. Mindful that *the Gap* can be narrowed, we work towards that end. Wants are motivating. They stir us into action and keep us going.

Wishes on the other hand are passive - all frustration and no action! Wishes that don't come true leave us in an unhappy place, feeling both unfulfilled and even less powerful than we would have been without the wish.

In the process of designing a full and satisfying life for ourselves, taking the time to be deliberate about the wants we choose is helpful. Our lives are time-limited, and our brains have no sense of priority. Only if we are 'minding' the brain, nudging it and directing its attention, can we help it to persist in making the changes which will optimise our chance to thrive. Fortunately, we have consciousness to help us. It's no accident that we call it a mind. Minding us is what it does.

Section 3: Narrowing the Gap

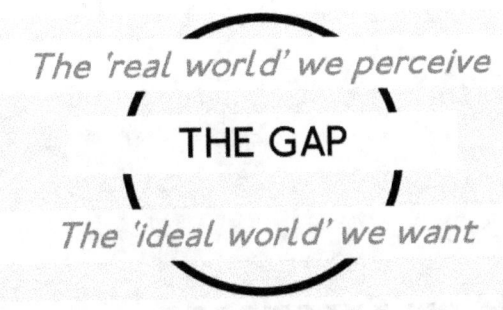

"He who fears he will suffer, already suffers because he fears."

Michel De Montaigne

"May your choices reflect your hopes, not your fears."

Nelson Mandela

"Responsibility...is...the ability to fulfill one's needs and to do so in a way that does not deprive others of the ability to fulfill their needs."

Dr. William Glasser

Ten

The World we Experience

How Real is what we Perceive?

As we live in *the Gap* between the real and the ideal - always trying to edge our perceptions closer to how we would like things to be - do we have any control of the 'real' side of this equation? Can we change what is out there in the world we experience, or are we helpless in the face of a reality that we can't control?

When faced by *the Gap,* it often appears that the 'real world' looms across our lives – intractable and inconvenient. What can we do with this apparently perverse 'reality' that will help us close *the Gap*? As we confront each of the *Gaps* that present themselves to us on the chequer board of life, is there anything we can do to change the 'reality' that we are comparing to our ideal?

The conundrum is that we can control <u>only</u> ourselves - and yet that confronting truth is both the problem and the solution. Because we can manage our mental processes, we are able to control the way they interpret information from the world around us. And, based on the perception that

Perceptions

results, we choose behaviours that form our capacity to understand and influence the world.

This means that we can not only choose the way we explain reality to ourselves, but we can also choose how to behave in order to adjust our own perceptions. If I perceive failing an exam as proof of my incapability, I might behave so as to avoid being tested again. If I interpret it as evidence that I have more to learn, I will work hard to improve my knowledge and skill. These two dimensions of self-management provide levers through which we can increase our choices and enhance our personal freedom. Both of these agencies of personal change are hinged on our understanding of the unreliability and malleability of perception.

Our Illusion of the World.

There almost certainly **is** a real world outside our own skin-covered self.[1] It's a world of people and events, natural and constructed objects; a world of colours, shapes and movement.

Our senses offer us information about this world. We can see and hear, touch and feel, taste and smell. These sensations provide the data that we use to make sense of the world, to keep ourselves safe and to live as contentedly as we can.

It's commonplace to describe what we perceive of the world as 'reality', implying that it is independent of our inner existence: but the 'otherness' of reality is a delusion. There is a real world. However, it is unlikely to be identical to the world of our perception.

---

[1] The existential conundrum: 'If a tree falls in the forest, but nobody sees it...' is not the one I want to address. George Berkeley (Irish philosopher) may have argued that what we can't perceive does not exist, but my point is practical, not philosophical - If our perceptions are interpreters of the energy we sense, then the instruments of interpretation are amenable to internal control.

Our sensory system is not designed to be the passive recipient of data. It's not like a camera or a sound-recording device. Our senses are more like translators, taking inputs from external sources and rendering them intelligible to the internal self. Just like the translator, they are interpreting, modifying, and making inferences from what they take in to help us understand and manage those inputs.

Our translators are 'built-in' to our perceptual system. They shape the information from outside us like a series of lenses. Like the lenses in our eyes, they play their part in making sense of the inputs that they encounter. Lenses change both what we see and what we are capable of seeing.

The Lenses of the Mind.

Our mental lenses are there to help us make sense of the data that we are receiving from external sources, in order to interpret it in ways that help us to manage ourselves in a world full of information. The information that we receive from the world *outside* our bodies crosses the threshold of our sensory system as energy, as waves of sound, light, or pressure that we have to interpret *inside* the container of skin that we inhabit. The lenses of the mind are there to interpret this avalanche of sensory data.[2] We can only process a very small percentage of the incoming 'information' (much less that 0.1%), so we have to ignore or guess at the missing data. At the same time, we have to *interpret* it by transforming the energy from light and sound waves detected by our sensory receptors into chemical and electrical messages that enter the brain and can be detected by the conscious mind.

So what are the lenses of the mind – and where do we get them from?

---

[2] It's estimated that a waking human being is bombarded by 11 million bits of sensory data per second, but is only able to process about 50 bits per second.

Perceptions

The Self-Created Lenses.

Some of our mind's lenses are moulded by our genes. However, most of them we create ourselves.

What we are perceiving today we filter through the lenses of our past experience. We interpret events by referring to our memories and thoughts about similar occurrences. We colour our understanding with the attitudes and values that we have acquired up to this point in our lives. Our discernment is often skewed by the limitations of the language we use to describe events to ourselves - and by the pain or pleasure we have previously encountered in associated circumstances. We assemble our beliefs, our presuppositions, our values, and our imagining in order to make sense of the world and manage our passage through its complexities.

Each acquired lens influences the emergence of other lenses. Consequently, 'the truth of things' is constructed on mutually supportive ways of interpreting not only the content but also the meaning of the data that we take in through our senses.

In this way, our personal history, our acquired knowledge, and previous interpretations directly affect whatever we are perceiving now. They help us to ignore some sensory inputs completely, to put our personal spin on large amounts of 'information' and to approximate or make general assumptions about other incoming data.[3]

Much of what seems to be 'real' is different for each individual. What we perceive is not the world as it is, but our own internal representation of the changing backdrop of our own personal existence. We don't so much encounter reality directly as create a personal map of the material world

---

[3] Among the models of communication elucidated by NLP (Neuro-Linguistic-Programming) is the assertion that, in order to avoid being swamped by detail, we modify our perceptions in at least 3 ways: by **deleting** some information, by **distorting** many inputs and by making **generalisations** about what we are sensing.

in which we are immersed. As Alfred Korzybski[4] taught, the maps we create don't necessarily correspond with the territory that they purport to describe. Our maps are inside us: our best attempts to describe the world that exists on the outside.

In this space, in our personal charting of our unique representations of the existential world, the element of choice emerges.

If we are participants in the creation of our perceptions, and internal narrators of the external events in our lives, then we have the tools to modify our perceived 'reality' in ways that serve us best. That means that when we change our perceptions by noticing different features of the world, things can seem very different.

In a year of Covid-19 restrictions and lock-downs, if I pay attention to our lost freedoms, our separation from our children and grandchildren, and to the other limitations that this experience has imposed on my life, *the Gap* between what I want and what I am experiencing will seem huge. If I attend to the fact that my wife and I are safe and well, that I have been able to use this time away from work productively and remain hopeful about the prospect of fewer restrictions in the future, I am not faced with so large a *Gap*. The situation has not changed: what changes are the aspects of the world that I have chosen to focus on.

Similarly, if I applied for a job that I really wanted (something that was definitely an 'ideal' for me) but I was not successful at interview, I could view that 'reality' in two very different ways. One way of seeing the situation is that it demonstrated that a door has closed in my life. It means that I don't have the qualifications or the experience to secure my 'ideal job'. In conjunction with other experiences of similar lack of success I can perceive the experience as proof that my ambitions are unreasonable, and that my only choice is to limit my future aspirations. Alternatively, I can pay attention to some different information. I can focus on my knowledge

---

[4] Alfred Korzybski 'Science and Sanity', 1933. This expression 'The map is not the territory' was also made famous by Gregory Bateson.

Perceptions

that many application processes are unreliable, that there will be many more opportunities for similar work, and that there are ways in which I can continue to improve my qualifications. I do not need to abandon my 'ideal': I can focus on how to close *the Gap*. Once again there is no change to the objective reality (assuming there **is** such a thing), but **my** reality - how **I** view the situation - has shifted. Instead of an intractable roadblock, I am seeing the same situation as a temporary hurdle; as a speedbump in the passage of life.

Let me give you another very simple but important example:

How many times have you said to yourself: "I can't do that" and acted as if it were 'true'. It's an experience so commonplace as to be unremarkable. Self-perception is an omnipresent filter through which we view the world. At the moment we utter those words, we are referring to what we believe is a verifiable aspect of our map of the world.

Suppose I say to myself: "I can't play chess." The chances are that this is a conclusion I have reached as a result of a very small portion of my perceived experience. Perhaps chess looked complicated and difficult when my uncle tried to explain it to me; or perhaps someone whom I respected said to me: "Chess will be too difficult for you - you don't have that kind of mind."

If I interpret these inputs as a literal truth, chess is now filtered through my internal lenses and located in the cognitive 'too hard' category that colours my perception.

My representation of the world includes many examples of this kind of internal narrative. I infer from my interpretation of experience (which is rarely identical with the episode as seen by an observer) that something is inaccessible to me, or that someone is untrustworthy, or that events are 'good' or 'bad'.

In the specific instance described above, I have concluded that any attempt I make to play chess will result in failure. Failure is associated with unpleasant feelings, so I conclude that it would be unwise of me to have anything to do with chess!

Following the Script

Now I have learned a script. My perception of chess is automated. I utter this 'truth' without further examination: "I can't play chess."

Hearing this objectively, we might rightly judge that this is an example of a 'self-fulfilling prophecy'. When it's explained, it's clear how I learned that behaviour. In the cascade of external data tumbling through the portals of perception, it is easy to make a generalisation from little evidence. Our mission as mindful humans is to learn how to challenge that internal creation of reality: to change it in such a way that it alters both our internal experience and the externally observable reality.

There are ways to do this, and they both involve choice. As predicted a few pages back, one way is to explicitly question our thinking; the other way is to choose a behaviour that challenges the related pre-suppositions. Our choices are most effectively extended when we do both.

I can question the 'reality' that is embodied in my script. I acknowledge that, at the time it was created, the belief: "I can't play chess" was intended to protect me. It buffered me from potential disappointment and pain. However, when my own children come home from school wanting to know more about the game and asking if I can play chess with them, I can either stick to my script, or decide to change it.

When my children want to play chess with me, I can choose to abandon my habitual response. I can replace: "I can't play chess" with "I have never learned to play chess". This cognitive transformation is profound. Once I replace 'I can't' with 'I have not yet learned', the landscape of my *internal* reality shifts. When I begin to play chess with them, the *external* observable reality changes as well. I may play inexpertly at first, learning as I go along, but the reality has shifted. You can watch my first stumbling

Perceptions

attempts and then my developing competence and say with certainty: "Rob is playing chess." The script: 'Rob can't play chess' is no longer valid. By changing the map and by following the contours of my new map, I have altered the territory.

As my friend Richard often says, the most effective way to change your capabilities is to 'fake it until you make it': to act as if the change has already been made - so that it will be!

As I suggested, my chess example is simple and relatively trivial. Yet in a significant way it's not trivial at all. As we will discover, it's a template for the kind of choice and change that can liberate us from self-limitation and from self-imposed incapacity. Because we can pay attention selectively and can challenge our own interpretations of the external world, we can write new scripts for ourselves and abandon the old.

Once we accept that everything we regard as 'reality' is our own internal representation of something - interpreted and learned from incoming data - then we will always know that we have control. As I write this, the world is battling through yet another year of its attempts to manage the Coronavirus we call Covid-19. There is an external reality here. There is a virus circulating that makes people sick and from which many people have died. Yet we can notice that this 'truth' has an extraordinary number of interpretations! Covid-19 can be viewed as a hoax or a frightening threat; it can represent a political opportunity, a vast conspiracy, or a devastating impediment to normal life; it may generate profound depression or astonishing resilience. The reality of Covid-19 exists independently of us. What it means to us, how we deal with it, the attitude we take to it, are all illustrations of the internal reality we choose to experience.

This is not news. In 1890, William James wrote that: "The greatest discovery of my generation is that a human being can alter their life by altering their attitudes of mind".[5] Our attitudes are lenses. Like our

---

[5] William James: 'The Principles of Psychology' 1890

assumptions, presuppositions, and many of our beliefs, they were written into the script of our lives to serve us. We once found them useful. When they have outlived their utility we can let them go.

The way we interpret experience writes the script for our lives. Many individual and very personal scripts contain the pain and disappointments embedded in our personal history. Through our self-talk and self-imaging, we can read these unhelpful scripts back into the present moments of our lives and thereby limit both the present and the future.

We can choose to create a new script!

There is no logical or neurological imperative that prevents us from learning new and more useful behaviours; choosing more liberating thoughts. Habit is simply the well-worn cloak that we inherit from our past: grooves in the sandy slope of the brain - customary but not inevitable or irreversible.

Mind is the instrument that can redirect the scripts that were once useful to us and allow us to create and read from the pages of a new screenplay for our life. Recomposing the manuscript that we once leaned on, we can insert this new page into the narrative of our lives.

Our perceptions of the world change. They will have changed many times already. The future does not have to be an echo of the past. Although we are informed by external 'reality', we are not required to be limited by it. Our perceptions are the scenery that creates the backdrop of our life's journey. They are not chains to the past, nor are they a prophecy for the future.

Eleven

Avoidance Motivation

Moving Away from what you Want

Imagine taking up a map and a compass and, instead of choosing a direct passage to your destination, planning a route that avoids the places where you *don't* want to go.

Like the politician who made his reputation by walking backwards, it would certainly require a lot of effort and might even make headlines. However, if you actually want to arrive at a destination or achieve a goal it would be neither effective nor efficient. Choosing where **not** to go is, at best, a very circuitous way of getting closer to a desirable objective.

And yet, many of us find ourselves too easily on that tortuous pathway. Instead of pursuing the 'wants' in our lives, we become focused on avoiding the things that we don't want!

Avoiding the negative.

If we think for a moment about the mind's tenacious preoccupation with *the Gap* between the real and the ideal, the attraction of the 'don't want' is understandable. We perceive whatever threatens to increase *the Gap* as undesirable, and as actually or potentially painful. It may widen *the Gap*! Just as we are motivated by attempting to close *the Gap* between what we want and what we are experiencing, we are also motivated to avoid pain – to avoid widening *the Gap* even further. This is our auxiliary source of motivation, intended to protect us from harm. After all, we have to survive in order to thrive. Danger is to be avoided for good reason!

This 'away from' or avoidance motivation is natural but often unhelpful. We feel pleasure from need-satisfying experiences, not from experiences that keep us safe from harm. The urge to be safe, while very powerful, doesn't always contribute to our well-being. So while avoiding the painful or potentially harmful might protect us, it can't help us to actually close *the Gap*. It may prevent *the Gap* from widening but will not narrow it.[1]

Thriving Transcends Surviving

To borrow a metaphor from Lynn Sumida[2]: in the river of life, keeping our head just above water is not enough. We can focus on treading water so that we don't drown. We might stay afloat that way, but we will be surviving, not thriving. To thrive, to feel the satisfaction of a life fully

---

[1] Political commentary is outside the remit of this book. It may be noteworthy however to observe that voting against the person or policy that you disapprove of might very well lead to being represented by a candidate who stands for nothing!

[2] Lynn Sumida: 'Choice Theory: Opening the Door to a New Identity' www.miruspoint.com

Avoidance Motivation

lived, we have to pursue our genetic birthright: to narrow *the Gap* and to feel powerful, loving, and free.

The markers of quality in our ideal world are the experiences, relationships and achievements that we have chosen in order to satisfy our needs - those that close *the Gap* between the real and the ideal. Whatever efforts we expend to prevent *the Gap* from growing further are defensive; they do not bring us closer to the ideal. Treading water can never match the positive feelings and sense of being in control that we get from swimming powerfully.

The most debilitating aspect of pain-avoidance is that it takes our eye off the goal. Like the man walking backwards, we are facing away from what we want, under the illusion that it will eventually bring us closer to the ideal. Sealed in the same confusion as the restless motorcyclists in Thom Gunn's poem 'On the Move'[3], at least we are doing something. It's easy to delude ourselves that anything that does not increase *the Gap* will close it.

In actuality, the painful experiences that we are attempting to avoid by concentrating on what we don't want steer us away from satisfaction, not towards it. They take the risk out of potential disappointment, rejection, or failure. However, they don't move us towards success or satisfaction.

Steering away from potential pain hurts rather than helps, because it eases us into the shadows of helplessness and blocks our emergence into the light of well-being.

---

[3] *"At worst one is in motion and at best,*
Having no absolutes in which to rest,
one is always nearer by not keeping still."
An extract from 'On The Move', Thom Gunn: 'Collected Poems', 1993

The Two Faces of Motive

If our ideal is to be confident and capable, striving with purpose and determination paves our way to enhanced competence. Of course, every ideal pursued, every satisfaction aspired to, will encounter the risk of failure. However, with our innate capacity to learn and change, failure needs never be final, and is rarely calamitous. Resilience is shaped through our response to impediments, not by our avoidance of them. Trepidation and anxiety steer us away from the satisfaction of achieving the ideal.

The good news is that every fear that constrains us, each negative perception that we experience as a threat, contains the key to the real want - to the positive want.

Let's examine some specific examples of the two sides of our motivation to be powerful or competent. On the left side of the table are self-perceptions we are trying to avoid. On the right side are the positive aspirations we have for ourselves:

We are avoiding the negative perception of being:	*What we want is to perceive ourselves as:*
Frustrated, incompetent, failing, fragile, unsure, weak, unsuccessful, unimportant.	*Capable, competent, confident, skilled, respected, effective, strong, important.*

The 'don't want' is simply the negative face of the actual 'want'. There is always a positive want or ideal matching the negative perception that we are trying to avoid. Indeed, our moving 'away from' behaviours are energised by the potential for pain inherent in not achieving the ideal. However, in practice making avoidance our goal is unproductive. We can

Avoidance Motivation

only be closer to the ideal by pursuing it, by 'flipping'[4] from the negative perception to the positive preference in our ideal world.

Almost all the 'don't wants' that camouflage our positive motivation are related to fears that our needs will not, or cannot, be satisfied. In the table below, each of the needs is associated with both a negative perception and a 'flipped' positive want:

What we are attempting to avoid being is:	What we want is to perceive ourselves as:
Lonely, left out, isolated, rejected, unwanted, friendless, mistrusted, abandoned.	Loved, cared about, cared for, included, liked, connected, befriended, friendly, trusted.
Coerced, constrained, limited, obstructed, restricted, unwilling, dependent.	Free, in-control, autonomous, independent, willing, self-sufficient.
Bored, weary, uninterested, ignorant, foolish, unintelligent, unsuccessful, defeated, exposed.	Learning, growing, developing, curious, joyful, inspired, challenged, achieving.
Fearful, anxious, scared, threatened, intimidated, bullied, vulnerable, insecure, endangered.	Safe, secure, confident, protected, trusted, hopeful, courageous, determined, resilient.

The secret to our well-being is to 'flip' from avoiding the pain of not achieving the ideal (as listed on the left above) in order to focus on striving for the satisfactions displayed on the right.

---

[4] 'Flipping' is an expression coined by my colleague Judy Hatswell to describe this kind of positive reframing.

Whether we endeavour to avoid what we fear, or apply ourselves to achieve what we want, the amount of effort is about the same. 'Avoiding' takes at least as much energy as striving for success!

Slaying the Bogeyman!

What you may notice is that, in attempting to avoid the risk of what we fear, we are almost always steering ourselves towards an encounter with it. In trying to avoid anxiety, we become anxious. Fearing failure, we take few chances and consequently shun the risk implicit in learning and growing. We undermine our own potential to prosper through enhancing our capability or skill.

It is the irony of the human situation that our brain can easily trap us by protecting us. Its predisposition to keep us from harm deters us from forming the resolve to succeed, or from the commitment that we require to fill our lives with the quality that we crave. Fear of *the Gap* widening widens it! Shying away from the unpredictable jeopardizes the satisfaction we can only experience by pursuing the ideal. Predictably, we become what we fear! In attempting to evade the 'bogeyman', we blunder into his grasp.

We can, of course, slay the bogeyman. Negation has no power over a mind set on pursuing the ideal; one that is intent on satisfying our genetic needs. The mind's natural motivation to narrow *the Gap* between the real and the ideal will urge us on - if we allow it to do so. If we identify what we are avoiding and flip to the positive preference – from the 'don't want' to the 'want' – then our pursuit of the ideal will enhance our well-being.

Of course, that pathway will never be free of difficulties and potential deterrents. What we desire is attainable only through effort and risk.

Just a few hours before I wrote these lines I happened to be watching a stage of the 'Tour de France' cycling race on the television. It occurred to me, as I watched the sprinters at the head of the peloton charging towards

Avoidance Motivation

the finish line, that their activity is a metaphor for a life well-lived. Intense effort followed by an explosion of speed as they dash for the line is their chosen vocation. They are too focused on the elusive chance of reaching the line first to attend to the risks of their frantic pursuit. Knowing that the possibility of pain is ever-present, they eschew the comfort of safety to embrace the opportunity of success.

This kind of drive to close *the Gap* is known as 'approach motivation'. It's the natural way for the mind to bring us the satisfactions and internal rewards that are the focus of quality in our lives. Approach motivation keeps our eyes on our goals, undeterred by obstacles.

Approach motivation is our pathway as we endeavour to thrive. Trips and stumbles, disappointment and misfortune attend every life. But each of us is blessed by the events, people and moments of delight that are glimpses of quality – instants when *the Gap* closes and we are experiencing our dream of the ideal. Closing *the Gap*, and every attempt to do so, is what the brain is designed for. Our brain activity and mental processes are chiefly constructed to allow us to invoke the choices that enable us to progress. Even though it's a feature of the human existence that we must survive in order to experience satisfaction and joy, contentment rarely attends a life slanted towards protection.

Balance - knowing how to dance through the unsteady passages of life by taking the stumbles in our stride, while remaining poised for the next step - is a pre-requisite of well-being. Ever-present unease is not so useful; it keeps us in thrall to itself. An awareness of danger can keep us safe to pursue our potential, but avoidance is not the goal itself - it's only useful if it liberates us to feel well and happy. Even if we sometimes have to name our fear in order to flip to the 'want' that hides behind it, it is the pursuit of need-satisfaction that opens us to joy.

Twelve

Behave yourself!

Behaving

In his seminal work[1], William Powers drew attention to the purpose of our behaviour: we behave to control our perceptions. We do what we do in order to bring the world we perceive as close as possible to the world we want.

Our own behaviours are the practical tools we can apply to bring our perceptions and our wants closer together. We use the generic word **'behaviour'** to describe the things we can do that appear to us to have an effect on the real world. We behave in order to make things better for ourselves.

As babies, we soon learn that there are behaviours we can employ to change our perceptions of the 'reality' of the world into which we are born. We use our crying behaviours to get the attention and sustenance we want. As infants, we try tears and tantrums to change our parents' 'no' into 'yes'. As adults, we behave so as to acquire the things we want. We

---

[1] William T Powers: 'Behaviour, the Control of Perception'. 1973

Behaving

choose the actions, words, and bodily expressions to build relationships with people and to influence their ideas. Even though we cannot control other people, we can manage ourselves so that other people will respond to our wishes with actions that are pleasing to us.

Across the history of mankind, enthusiastic teachers have inspired their students to learn. The oratory and promises of politicians have persuaded people to elect them. The nurturing love of parents ushers their children towards responsibility and encourages the growth of capability. Through craft and ingenuity, we can bring new objects and technologies into existence. Therefore, there is a valid sense that we can change the world by controlling ourselves. Our behaviours **can** have an effect on other people and events, even though we cannot directly control anyone but ourselves.

Only a few of us are privileged to be a Shakespeare, an Einstein, or a Churchill - with the knowledge and influence that can enhance the lives of generations. Thankfully, most of us are also "forbade to wade through slaughter to a throne and shut the gates of mercy on mankind"[2] as did Hitler and Stalin. Although few of us will have the influence of Steve Jobs or Bill Gates, most of us influence in small ways, either for good or ill. But however great or limited our sphere of influence, none of us can actually 'control' the world or people around us in the same way in which we control ourselves.

It is through the agency of the changes that we make in ourselves that we can have an effect on the world that we discern. Those behaviours, our **own** behaviours, are all we can control. With our own behaviours we can influence what we perceive to be 'out there'.

---

[2] From 'Elegy Written in a Country Church Yard', Thomas Gray, 1751

The Gratuitous Admonition

There are some curious uses of the word 'behave'. Among my earliest memories are the words and tone of voice of my mother and my teachers as they admonished me for conduct that they viewed as undesirable. "Behave yourself" they would say!

At the time, I was quite familiar with those words. I heard them often. I still hear people use that strange expression. The words 'behave yourself' uttered in a reproving tone are part of a linguistic shorthand that means 'do as I want you to do'!

On the face of it though, it is a meaningless admonition. I was always 'behaving myself'. I still am. When I stop behaving, I will be dead!

When I am behaving, I am doing many things that are predicated by my existence as a human organism. I cannot *not* behave! To be human and alive is to be immersed in an unremitting procession of behaviours that extends through time and space, marking the passage of my mortality. At any time in my life, I may be talking, listening, thinking, acting, feeling, running, walking, sitting, sleeping, enjoying, fearing, aching, tensing, relaxing ... the catalogue of the ways in which I may be behaving is long and varied. I am always behaving, and every behaviour involves the coordinated experience of **thought** and **action**, **physiology** and **emotion**.

The Four Elements of Behaviour

Whatever I am doing to create an 'output' initiated by my brain will have four components: there will always be action and thought, feelings and a physiological state.

If you were watching me at this moment, you would say that I was writing, but all four components of behaviour are present (though not all are visible). As I am typing on my laptop, I am simultaneously composing,

Behaving

sitting upright, and feeling the customary mixture of anticipation and trepidation as I watch the words appearing on the screen. Writing, like every behaviour, involves **thought** and **feeling**, with a **body state** that supports my **actions**.

William Glasser[3] used the expression 'total behaviour' to describe the simultaneous occurrence of these four elements of every behaviour: **thought, action, physiology,** and **emotion**. He used the very practical metaphor of the wheels of a car to illustrate the relationship between the four elements of behaviour, noting that we commonly have a high degree of control over our actions and thoughts (the front wheels), but only indirect control over our feelings and physiology (the back wheels). Indirectly, we can change our feelings with different thinking, and change our physiology through actions; but very few of us can change the 'back wheels' by an act of will alone.

Whether our control is direct or indirect, our ability to manage and change our behaviours is intrinsic to the effectiveness of the four 'wheels' of our behavioural system. Because they occur concurrently, changing any one element of our behaviour changes them all. If we change our actions, our feelings, thoughts, and physiology will match the new action.

The sage advice of many generations is validated by this interplay between the four elements of our car:
~ Am I feeling tense or angry? - deep breaths will calm me.
~ Am I paralysed by thinking obsessively about having so many things to do? - do one thing at least. Start with any action and get moving.
~ Am I overwhelmed by the events of the day? - a walk on the beach or in any other natural environment will help me regain perspective.

Whenever we are feeling stuck or sad, there is usually an element of behaviour that we can activate so as to improve the situation.

---

[3] Of the many contributions Dr. Glasser made to our understanding of the human mind, the metaphor of the car, with the four wheels that represent the four dimensions of behaviour, was the one he believed was the most helpful.

Behaviours put us in the Driver's Seat

This interplay of our behavioural options helps us to steer our lives. Each of the components of our behavioural 'car' is different, but each is yoked to the others by neurological necessity. Knowing this offers us far greater consciousness of control than we would otherwise seem to have.[4] When any one of the elements of behaviour is not helping us to narrow *the Gap*, we can choose to focus on a different one. By changing my thinking I can initiate new actions: take actions that will alter my thoughts and feelings; or shift to a more alert physiology by noticing the urgency of my tasks.

Without this interplay of the elements of behaviour we would lack the flexibility which makes humans so adaptable. We are able to manage obsessive thoughts, immobilising feelings, and ineffective action by activating a different element of behaviour. Actors on the stage of life, we can attend to the reaction of the 'audiences' to whom we play, and then change our acting to elicit the response we seek. When they are needed, shifts in our thinking can transport us to a different perspective, or focus our attention on another of our many wants.

Even though we have this capability to change our behavioural 'wheels', this control is not automatic. We have to learn to take advantage of this behavioural flexibility and engage the determination in order to activate this potential. It is alarmingly easy to get stuck - to repeat an action we know is not working long after it is not helping us. That's the nature of the brain. Because our neural learning automates our behaviours, we often keep using behaviours that are not useful to us. As we have noted, we can change these habits of mind - but not easily. The grooves in the cerebral sand often run deep, trapping us in the habits we have constructed even when we don't like where they are taking us.

Remember, almost all of our vast repertoire of behaviours is embedded in automated patterns that we initiate and execute without conscious

---

[4] Because the car is such an accessible metaphor, we can teach our children to use it quite early in their lives.

Behaving

thought. The brain runs our lives by doing what it has always done. To distract it from its habitual repertoire requires a conscious nudge and a commitment to learn and use new pathways.

So it's commonplace to keep doing things that don't work for us, or that even prolong our discontent. The 'habit brain' can persist with learned behaviours even when they are of no use to us. The human capacity for spinning the wheels in a familiar rut is ever-present, but not helpful.

However, we can change our 'state' - our total behaviour - when we harness our mind's ability to alter the course of our brain's activity. The behavioural system's capacity for adaptability is there to help us. The four wheels of our behaviour car provide alternatives, so long as we pay attention to them and expend the effort required to change. To utilise our potentially immense suite of behaviours we have to pay mindful attention to what is happening to us in the present moment.

We can, when we choose, respond mindfully to *the Gap*. We can identify and abandon unhelpful thinking, acting, feeling or physiology and change our actions or thoughts to those that offer greater need-satisfaction. Whatever 'state' we are experiencing, our ability to observe ourselves in that state and to change our thoughts and commence different actions is always present.

The brain can be redirected by consciously attending to what is happening and then identifying and implementing different behaviours. When my writing becomes laborious, when I am feeling dull and uninspired, I can slip on my walking shoes and head out for a period of brisk exercise. Within minutes, my physiology will be different, and quite often my 'stuck' thoughts will begin to flow again. When I feel the discomfort of anger stirring in my emotions, directing my consciousness to become an observer enables me to stand aside from whatever is disturbing me and control my voice and physiology to let go of the growing tension.

When I worked with young people - teenagers who were only just beginning to learn mastery of their behavioural system - I would often insist that we walk and talk together in order to help them change from an unresourceful state to a more useful one. As soon as a change is made to one element of behaviour, the others are also altered.

Paying Attention to Ourselves

As we learn to observe our brain in action, we can predict our own automated responses. Our brain and mind at their best enable us to respond creatively to the rhythm of life, adapting to its changes and challenges - by learning to cope with the unexpected pauses and discordant notes that threaten our contentment. Remember that we are always living in *the Gap*. From moment to moment, we choreograph our lives in response to the space between the real and the ideal. We do what we can to mind *the Gap*: to enhance our well-being and minimise the effects of misfortune.

We do this best when we have a wide repertoire of behaviours to call on. The 'Law of Requisite Variety'[5] tells us that in any situation the part of the system with most flexibility will control the system; the person in the system with the most adaptability will have the greatest control of their own experience. Being open to change and experimentation serves us well. We are liberated when we know and understand that we can escape the leaden-footed grasp of ill-being by pursuing a new behaviour, rather than persevering with what is not helping.

This is the advantage of knowing 'the music of the mind' – of understanding the working of the brain and mind that together orchestrate our behaviours. When we know that the brain serves our survival - always doing its best to enhance the well-being of the body it serves - we can recognise and learn the practices that will help us to feel in control. We are then liberated to use the brain's resources to achieve contentment. Knowing that the miracle of mind provides us with awareness - enabling us to anticipate and interpret the imperfect attempts of our neural networks

---

[5] The 'Law of Requisite Variety' is derived from the Science of Cybernetics, and in particular from the work of W.R. Ashby.

Behaving

and deftly correct them - we have the tools to construct our own well-being.

All around us, the world assails our perceptions with the vicissitudes of existence. We are not guaranteed happiness. There is no genetic instruction that writes contentment into the narrative of our lives. Suffering and difficulty are strangers to no-one. Life drizzles problems into the landscape of every existence. We are not buffered against adversity by wealth or intellect. However, because we have the resources of our mind to guide the creative brain from which consciousness emerges, we can summon the resilience to emancipate ourselves.

The theme of this publication is that we can manage *the Gap* that is our genetic legacy. Minding it through understanding and acceptance makes such a difference. Consciousness of *the Gap* and the part it plays in our lives can be our privilege: the key to making helpful choices. If we spend time wishing circumstances were different, we easily tire. If we choose acceptance, we can thrive.

As we increasingly understand and accept that it is the feeling of frustration brought about by *the Gap* that is the source of our motivation - our ability to make choices - we can be grateful for this gift to our humanity. We are not creatures who simply react as automatons to events around us. We have volition. We can choose the behaviours with which we mind *the Gap*.

Our will is not forged from genetic certainty but from the inherited capacity to make choices; to put a unique stamp on the ways in which we experience our being. Through choices we can change. Knowing and utilising the complexity and capacity of our behavioural system enables us to exploit and enhance the control system that is ourselves.

Section 4: Shaping the Gap

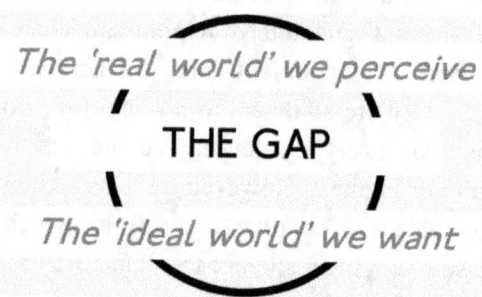

*"You are fettered," said Scrooge, trembling. "Tell me why?"
"I wear the chain I forged in life," replied the Ghost.
"I made it link by link, and yard by yard;
I girded it on of my own free will, and of my own free will
I wore it."*

Charles Dickens

"It is almost impossible for anyone, even the most ineffective among us, to continue to choose misery after becoming aware that it is a choice."

William Glasser

"Good or bad, everything we do is our best choice at that moment."

William Glasser

Thirteen

Relationships and the Brain

The Strongest Need?

Relating is what we do. Humans are creatures for whom the establishment of inter-personal ties is both a survival advantage and an avenue of meaningful experience.

One of the fastest growing areas of scientific study examines how the brain connects with and is influenced by other brains. This is what Daniel Siegel[1] describes as 'the neurobiology of **we**'. From this area of study we know that the brain has specialised structures that prepare us for a social life: our own brains learn from observing and interacting with other brains. These structures can help us to be deeply intuitive about when to trust and whom to trust. They can guide us or misguide us, so it helps to know that they are at work.

The need for relatedness is genetic. Our genes urge us to love, to belong, to be included and connected. We are born with the means to learn how to satisfy this need: to create and sustain relationships. We learn that

---

[1] Daniel Siegel: 'The Neurobiology of We' 2008.

smiling attracts other people and that their attention benefits us. We understand, long before we can name this behaviour as 'smiling', that this is one way of securing the attention of other people.

Our perceptual system detects the energy emanating from other individuals and we translate that vitality into information about them. Some behaviours create the energy that draws people together. Other behaviours send signals that generate suspicion or hostility. Getting these indicators right is important for our well-being.[2]

Very early in our lives we learn that behaviours such as smiling, eye contact, welcoming facial expressions and paying attention to other people attract them. As we mature and build on these foundation skills, we acquire a collection of the behaviours that enable us to connect with others and foster satisfying relationships.

Because our connections with each other occupy the heart of our perception of being, the need to create and tend satisfying relationships is a necessity.[3] Being cared about, loved, feeling included, or belonging - these connected experiences are almost universally important. We are, by nature, relaters. One of the significant markers of human well-being is tied to satisfying relationships.

We do experiment with the usefulness of disconnecting behaviours. As babies, we were born with the capacity to express anger; we use crying and other distress behaviours to get attention when we feel hungry or uncomfortable. This seems to work well until the age at which we learn to distinguish ourselves from the people around us. Then most of us gradually notice that these signals of anger may get attention but can also damage relationships. Of course, by the time we are in a position to choose

---

[2] One of the many impediments suffered by people with autism (Autism Spectrum Disorder) is the difficulty they have in decoding these interpersonal signals.

[3] Dr William Glasser went so far as to maintain that almost all human unhappiness is the result of unsatisfying relationships.

Relationships and the Brain

connecting rather than disconnecting behaviours, the latter have often become habits. When we turn to these habits in our adult life, they are rarely helpful.

The Pleasure that Brings Pain

The need for relationships, for love and connection, occupies a prime position in every kind of media. It is the stuff of heart-breaking tales and heart-warming movies. Because of the strong emotional nature of relationships, they generate drama and tears as well as extraordinary bonds and lifetime connections.

The connections between our relationships and our well-being open us to a curious contradiction. Although relating is naturally satisfying, the way we manage our relationships can lead us towards pain and unhappiness when we get it wrong. If relating to others is in our genes, why do many of us put it into practice so imperfectly?

As we explore the world of relationships, knowledge about which behaviours connect and which disconnect is gradually accumulated. We expand our repertoire of the behaviours that will help us to relate well to others. We also learn how to deliberately discourage connections (and often use this behaviour rather cruelly with our peers).

Every individual or group I have ever worked with can name the behaviours that build connections, and those that can damage them. However, although we have the **knowledge** about how to nurture satisfying relationships, we don't always put this knowledge into practice. Our self-orientation and our other genetic needs lead us astray at times. We damage the ties to others thoughtlessly when we pay too much attention to ourselves.

Our problem is that the proclivity for selfishness is also designed into our genes through the needs for power and freedom! These needs push us apart and are essential to our existence as individuals. This inevitable conflict between our competing needs for power and autonomy and our need to connect and relate is awkward to manage. Getting our own way or going our own way we feel powerful and free – but these are disconnecting behaviours.

The result is that sustaining any kind of relationship is effortful and challenging, even for a well-managed mind. In relating to someone else, *the Gap* intrudes often. The reality of being an individual is often at odds with our attempts to make connections with others.

The Contradictions of Connection

One of the reasons why relationships can heal us or hurt us - eliciting either profound pleasure or debilitating distress - is that the experience of being connected is somewhat illusory. Because we are individuals, behaving as if we are joined can be confusing. We might connect easily. Sustaining the connection is more difficult.

The brain begins by drawing us on. Somewhat controversial research has led to the hypothesis that we have specialised nerve cells that enable us to detect the energy arising from whatever another person is doing or feeling. As a result, we seem to experience the same feelings as we would if we were doing these things ourselves. These 'mirror neurons' are particularly active in the initial stages of relating to, loving, or befriending another individual. They help us to feel connected.[4]

When we have these feelings of rapport, it's as if we are actually connected to another person, but what we are experiencing is in fact parallel activity in two separate brains. Each person in a relationship is connected through their own *internal* experience. It's the energy arising

---

[4] As I write, the existence of 'mirror neurons' and the part they play in our ability to develop rapport with another person is controversial. There is some scientific evidence that suggests that the mind's capacity for empathic connection can be wholly explained by the interpretive ability of our perceptual system.

Relationships and the Brain

from the internally-generated feelings that is detected and reciprocated by the other person.

In the relationship experience, the satisfaction is derived through the felt connection with another person. When our internal control system feels this strong connection to someone else, the feeling of unity is satisfying. But because the other person is really an independent control system, they are not actually 'one with' us, even though we might feel as if they are. And being an independent control system, they are not under our control.

What poses a potential threat to every relationship is that, while we *feel* connected to each other, we are always individuals. Our need for relatedness brings us together but can never create a single identity: our needs for power and autonomy play their part in keeping us separate. The need to relate brings us together. The needs to be powerful and free push us apart.

Expectation Generates Disappointment

One of the stumbling blocks to sustaining satisfying relationships is that many interpersonal ties come with an unrealistic expectation. *The Gap* that we expected to close completely doesn't! The ideal of 'we-ness' that we expect to be achieved remains elusive.

Whether the relationship is with a romantic partner, a friend, or a colleague it's easy to confuse the behaviour of the other person with the health of the relationship. The rapport that was established creates the expectation that we will think alike and want the same things. With this thinking, if we perceive that whatever the other person does or says falls short of **our** internal sense of what is ideal, then the relationship is often adversely affected. We confuse *The Gap* between **the other person's** behaviour and **our** ideal with *the Gap* between **our** behaviour and **our** ideal. The mind is easily misled into trying to close a *Gap* that arises through behaviour that is not in our control - as if it were. The error signal is there, but not the capacity to correct it.

Of course, this rarely happens early in the relationship. In the early stages of friending, loving, or learning to work with and appreciate someone else, we stretch our personal boundaries to include the other.[5] Our mental energy is applied to the 'we' - the things we have in common - or to those which complement each other.

However, as the relationship progresses, we become increasingly aware of differences. The dissimilarities in personality and the individual characteristics of each person in the relationship become clearer. These emerging differences can feel like a threat to the relationship itself.

When this happens, we have choices. On the one hand, there is an opportunity to appreciate the differences between us. When we can appreciate the qualities of the other person, the relationship is strengthened. Realising that we are two individuals, we can enjoy the variety of preference and belief that enriches the relationship. Alternatively, we can succumb to the temptation to reduce the differences by attempting to improve or 'fix' the other person. Unfortunately, the second choice is common.

Because, initially, our apparent sameness seemed so important to our connection, acceptance of difference is challenging. As our dissimilarities become clearer, and perhaps intrusive, it's normal to experience an urge to close the widening separation between the other person and **our** ideal of perfection. We can succumb to the temptation of doing our best to 'make' the other person more like us. We try to close *the Gap* by eliminating the differences between us. Not realising the futility of our efforts, we attempt to control their behaviours. We try to mend them. As a result, we both become miserable!

---

[5] In 'The Road Less Travelled' 1978, Scott Peck describes this process as cathexis – the focus of our mental energy on another person to the extent that it seems to collapse the boundaries between us.

Relationships and the Brain

The Third Entity

With mindful self-awareness, we can notice what we are doing and recognise the foolishness of the impulse to reshape the other person in the image of ourselves. By paying attention to the irrationality of our own mind, we can catch it in the act of blaming or complaining and resist the temptation to do so.

Blaming the other person, complaining about their behaviour, and treating them with less kindness and respect than we formerly did, are commonplace in the deteriorating stages of a relationship. After all, we reason, **I** am the same, so it must be the behaviour of the other person that is creating stress in our relationship!

What this commonplace thinking does not take into account is that every relationship consists of three entities, not just two. The energy that each of us generated in connecting with each other is like the third entity in every relationship. It's the glue, the vitality, that holds us together. In every relationship there are the two people involved, connected by a third entity - the relationship itself. The relationship is not a person - it's the energy that connects us and the respect that we show in nurturing that energy. The crucial essence of a successful relationship is what happens between us: how we treat each other, the signals that we send and interpret, the tolerance and understanding with which we manage our differences, the respect we show for the unique separateness of the other.

An insight that is significant in almost all relationships is simply stated: 'We can like or love each other without *being like* each other'!

It is this third dimension of the relationship that is damaged when we are no longer getting along with each other as we used to. *The Gap* we experience may seem as if it is the fault of the other, but often it is not. The irritation we begin to experience at the other's individuality is internally generated. *The Gap* between our ideal of the relationship and our deteriorating perception of it can only be narrowed by repairing the relationship itself – by addressing the way we get along with each other, by the kindness and tolerance we are prepared to show each other, and by the ways in which we express our regard for each other.

This part of the relationship dynamic - what develops between us - is a shared responsibility in which each person is totally responsible for their own share. We can control our own behaviours and our share of the third entity. We can't control the behaviour of the other person or their contribution to the relationship. When we try to overstep the boundaries and control what is the other person's responsibility, we enter the cycle of blame.

Fourteen

Finding Fault

Blaming: Familiar but Unproductive

Thinking that another person is responsible for our own internal state brings attendant complications to any relationship. It is one of the three dysfunctional behaviours that the mind suggests to us when a relationship is not going well. As long as we cling to the assumption that our internal states come from outside ourselves, finding someone or something to blame seems natural. Whether the relationship is within the family, with a colleague, friend, or acquaintance, locating the problem outside ourselves is a frequent temptation.

When we are not getting along with another person, or when the circumstances attending our relationship appear to us to be far from the ideal, we can be tempted to:

- ... Blame the other person and accuse them of hurting us in a way that inflicts pain on our internal state.
- ... Complain that we are the victims of events or circumstances for which the other person is responsible.
- ... Make excuses for our own behaviours based on our conviction that they were caused by someone else.

> ... Believe and expect that someone else, or some new event, can and should intervene to excuse us from responsibility.

Of course, this is misleading. The 'other' in any relationship may do something that does not please us. However, the pleasure or pain we experience describes what is going on inside us; it is not something that they are doing. Their action is separate from our displeasure, and it is something that we interpret and evaluate inside our own mind.

The same brain mechanisms that help us to connect with other people and mirror their feelings can easily mislead us. Because what is happening inside me may coincide with another person's behaviour, it's very easy to conclude that one is 'causing' the other - that the other person is intentionally behaving in order to upset me. Then it's a simple step to hold them responsible for my feelings and to blame them and complain about them; to see myself as a victim of their actions. When this happens, the brain structures that support interpersonal connection turn back upon themselves to damage our relationship.

One way to be clear about these situations is to think about where the problem or the discontent is located. If the frustration signal is in me, it's my responsibility to find a solution. Trying to outsource the solution to the problem to the other person, by blaming them and expecting them to fix it, will lead to distress for both of us.

Finding fault with them will not solve my problem or improve things. Blaming and complaining are an existential threat to our relationship – to the way in which we are relating to each other. As Stephen Karpman[1] pointed out, these are elements of a triad of unhelpful behaviours that activate and perpetuate dysfunction in a relationship.

---

[1] Stephen B Karpman: 'A game-free life' 2014 (and many other articles). A model that describes the dysfunctions in personal relationships created when power games erode personal responsibility. In trying to evade responsibility we blame or complain about another person and make excuses for ourself.

Finding Fault

The way out of this triangle of hurt is to take responsibility for the only aspects of the relationship that we can control. We can control our own choice of behaviours. We have control of our own contribution to the relationship (including a decision to end it). However, if the relationship is important to us, then the way in which we are relating to the other person is our responsibility. The pain we feel when things are not going well is our own pain. We have zero control over the other person, or of their contribution to the relationship. It is our attempt to control the other person with criticism or blame that is damaging.

Remember that we are an internal control system. We can control our own choices. We can, and should, take 100% responsibility for our own preferences, for behaviours that will sustain our relationships. Attempting to close *the Gap* between the real and the ideal through futile attempts to control the behaviour of our friend, partner or colleague will inevitably make things worse.

Even when we act in the name of love, any attempt to change each other will be felt as coercive. All our attempts to 'fix' the other person in the relationship will founder on the rocks of **their** genetic needs.

Understanding

If we are prepared to accept responsibility for our own behaviours in all of our relationships, it's not difficult to identify the thoughts and actions that are most likely to sustain and strengthen the way in which we relate to each other.

Almost every person can easily name the behaviours that strengthen our connections with another person or group. We can also accurately identify the words and actions that will harm the relationship. We have this information - but we often don't act on what we know.

If we want to relate well to another person, chief among the skills that support a productive connection is listening for understanding. Really listening! Through listening and paying attention, understanding and appreciation emerge.

Listening is effortful. To really listen to each other with full attention, trying our best to go beyond hearing in order to understand and appreciate the meaning behind the words, requires a commitment of energy and time. When we listen to each other attentively, we are communicating our respect for the differences between us and exhibiting our positive regard for the other. The act of listening entails acceptance of difference - the recognition and affirmation of our separateness.

As well as listening, if we demonstrate care and concern; encourage and trust the other person; respect our differences and negotiate them with an open mind, then we will be making our contribution to sustaining the relationship. It's not a difficult formula. It won't actually guarantee that we succeed in our quest to keep the connection strong – that may depend on the reciprocal contributions of the other person – but it is what **we** can do. Controlling their response is what we can't do!

The emphasis is (has to be) that every healthy relationship is grounded by mutual recognition of the unique and separate selves involved. A productive and need-satisfying relationship will remain healthy if each of the individuals in the relationship is liberated to be themselves; to be the best each of them can be, when they respect each other as autonomous individuals co-existing in a satisfying relationship.

Allow Spaces in your Relationship[2]

Our reflective self knows that if either person in a relationship attempts to control the other, then friction is inevitable. Together, our genetic need for

---

[2] Kahlil Gibran, Lebanese poet: "Let there be spaces in your togetherness" – 'The Prophet' 1923.

Finding Fault

autonomy and the parallel need we all share to be personally powerful, orchestrate our strong rejection of attempts at a take-over.

The brain is designed to resist invasion. It immediately identifies any attempt to do our thinking for us as a threat. In the face of this perceived danger to our urge to be self-sufficient, we usually activate the emotional brain and fight or freeze: push back through dissent, or close down.

When we excuse our own attempts to change the other person in any relationship by pointing to the ways in which we perceive that they are falling short of our ideal, we are subtly distorting the nature of human motive. We all behave to close *the Gap* between **our** perceptions of the real and **our** conceptions of the ideal. That divide is our internal motive. Comparing **my** ideal with my perceptions of **your** reality does create frustration - but that frustration is only **within me**. All our mental processes are internal. We can't delegate responsibility for closing our *Gap* to someone else!

Similarly, when we try to treat a relationship as though it were a transaction: when I choose to like, love or approve of you, or to be kind and respectful towards you only when you behave in a certain way, then the 'you' in the relationship is diminished or negated.

If my regard for you is conditional - only activated if you are a certain kind of person or do certain things – I am acting as though only one person in the relationship counts.

A satisfying relationship is not a transaction. As individuals, we always have choices about our own thoughts and actions. I can be kind, helpful and supportive even if *you* are not. The energy that flows between us - the energy that creates the relationship - is not dependent on either sameness or obedience; it is forged by the respectful ways in which we relate to each other and the space we allow for each other to satisfy their own needs in their own way.

Choosing our Way

Many of the decisions we make in leading our own lives are ones we make for 'selfish' reasons. We do what we do because it makes sense to us; because it is personally need-satisfying.

For most of my life, I have been, one way or another, in the 'people business'. As a colleague and as a leader, I know that the contribution of others is essential to my own effectiveness and achievement. Consequently, I attend to the research that tells me that a huge percentage of my success when working with other people comes from the quality of the relationships I form with them.[3] I try to get along with people, to respect the ways in which they are different from me. The more I focus on what the other person's uniqueness brings to our work together, the easier I find it to appreciate them.

I am sometimes accused of being naive or too forgiving of people who are trying to get their own way. I am asked why I don't see that such people are being selfish or manipulative. It's suggested that this should be a reason for not liking them, or not trusting them.

Accusing me of being gullible is wide of the mark though. The truth is the opposite. I expect everyone to be self-serving. Some people are better at disguising their self-focus than others!

It follows, from the theory of human behaviour espoused in these pages, that most people will strive to gratify their own needs. The psychology of internal control explains to us that everyone is motivated to get what **they** want, to be guided by the ways that they have learned to satisfy their genetic predispositions, and to avoid what hurts them.

---

[3] Research conducted by Harvard University, the Carnegie Foundation and Stanford Research Centre all concluded that 85% of job success comes from having well-developed soft skills (people skills), and only 15% of job success comes from technical skills and knowledge (hard skills).

Finding Fault

Because I choose to expect this, I am not disappointed when people look after themselves and promote their self-interest. The people around me who express disappointment with their friends or family, co-workers or bosses, are the ones showing their own lack of insight. They are holding other people to an inappropriate standard of perfection. Everyone's brain is designed to serve and protect themselves – not someone else. Our minds are inclined to mind us first!

Now, I am not saying that people are never generous, supportive, helpful, and altruistic. Of course they are. What I am saying is that they take pleasure in those laudable behaviours. Our internal processing does not exist in isolation: we live social lives. When we understand that it serves us to be tolerant and understanding, we can fine-tune our behaviours to do what is socially responsible and enjoy doing so.

A very blunt (but very shrewd) mentor offered me a nugget of wisdom when I was a young teacher.[4] Ever since that day, his pithy response on hearing me express dislike of a colleague has been a priceless touchstone of tolerance and acceptance. In his soft Yorkshire accent he said bluntly: "Not liking people is an excuse for treating them badly."
I have often found myself musing on the truth of his remark. It has much to do with unhappiness in the world: from tribal conflict and the justification of atrocities, to smouldering disputes between groups and even within families. The brain's fallacious association of 'not understanding' with 'not liking' bedevils many relationships in its unhelpful assumption. It hurts those who are 'not liking' and those who are 'not liked' almost equally.

I find it helpful to think of this kind of disconnection as energy wasted and discontent multiplied. Whatever other people do, wherever they are placed

---

[4] Malcolm Fidgeon was a school Head Teacher. He was also the London football scout for Manchester United for many years - David Beckham was among those whom he signed up for United. His funeral in 2005 was attended by many footballers and former colleagues whose lives were influenced by this wise and remarkable man.

on **my** continuum of pleasure and pain, responding with dislike or playing tit-for-tat harms me. It is a distraction. *The Gap* is widened to no good purpose.

Rule out Rules!

In the midst of making sense out of the muddle of living, we often make 'rules' for ourselves. Identified by 'must' and 'ought', 'should' and 'have to', these mandates infiltrate our thinking. They become the means by which we filter our perceptions through our own valuing. As trusted perceptions of 'how things should be', they define and buttress the ideal that is one pole of *the Gap*. They can create, as Albert Ellis[5] observed, unreasonable self-expectations. Even when they help us to be clear about what we want, rules are at best an inflexible way of defining the ideal; at worst they pervade our lives with intolerance.

Applying a rule that we have made for ourselves to other people's behaviour is an attribution error. If it suits us, we are free to make rules for ourselves. Applying our rules to other people simply increases the uncomfortable space between the real and the ideal that is our constant companion. The more we narrow the scope of the ideal by prescribing it with specifics, the harder it is to feel content. Moreover, when we create the conditions (the rules that will define *the Gap*), we position ourselves as captives to the action of another. When I allow myself to be disturbed by another person's behaviour, I have handed over the keys to my citadel of well-being. I am in thrall to what I describe as someone else's 'bad' behaviour.

---

[5] Albert Ellis developed Cognitive Behaviour Therapy to help his clients deal with irrational beliefs that were limiting or harming them. These 12 irrational beliefs include: 'Everyone should love and approve of me'; 'When things do not go the way I wanted and planned, it is terrible'; 'People who do bad things should be punished severely'.

Finding Fault

That's why choosing tolerance, forgiveness and forbearance are so useful for our well-being. They are minders of *the Gap*. By stretching the boundaries of acceptance, they diminish the separation of the real from the ideal. Not only do they preserve and nurture relationships, but they also make it easier to live a mindful and satisfying life.

Fifteen

Choosing Misery?

If our Choices are so Powerful, how did I end up Miserable?

Can it possibly be true that misery is a choice?

Without a mental life, we could not be the resourceful, adaptable creatures that we are. Having a mind defines who and what we are as humans. Given this, is there any way of making sense of the idea that we choose the maladies of the mind? Is it possible that we choose misery, depression, and other psychological afflictions?

The simple answer to this question is NO – we don't choose to be miserable. Feeling miserable is not in our ideal world.

The more complicated answer - the answer that is much more difficult to accept if you are experiencing the symptoms of any kind of psychological distress - is that YES, the unhappiness we are experiencing *can be* the result of choices we have made or are making.

Choosing Misery

Notice how carefully I phrased that last statement. Of course, we don't decide: 'I want to be unhappy.' The brain chooses pleasure rather than pain. However, it's one of the ironies embedded in the way that we accumulate our neural connections, and in which our mind learns and develops, that we can unwittingly create some aspects of our own distress.

The two questions we might ask ourselves are: 'Where do pain and distress come from?' and 'Why do we find it so hard to let them go?'

Five Prologues to Pain

The precursors of psychological distress often seem to come from the outside, from the behaviour of other people or external events. However, the pain is always experienced inside. The external perceptions are the harbingers of an imminent problem, not the causes of it. For example, consider these 5 precursors of distress:

1. When somebody or something in our Quality World is suddenly no longer there. This might be a relationship break-up or the death of someone close to us, or the disappointment of a goal denied, or even an opportunity missed. Naturally enough, we grieve for the sudden absence of something or someone that has been important to us. We routinely build our lives around narrowing *the Gap*. The sudden absence of an important inner motive and the change in our personal world is an occasion for grief.

2. Someone whom we are attempting to control is resisting. As discussed in Chapter Thirteen, attempting to impose our control over someone else is mostly futile and almost always generates strong resistance. However, if we conclude that we can't be happy unless the other person changes, we try to close *the Gap* we perceive by changing them. My control system versus your control system never works out well! Consciously trying to impose your will on another person is, whether we realise it or not, making the choice to be miserable.

3.   Similarly, when we rely on the love and approval of other people for our own well-being, we can feel unhappy when they don't supply it. The habit of looking outside of ourselves for need-satisfaction can be a hangover from a childhood expectation of compliance[1], or acquired later in life in order to avoid taking responsibility for our own well-being. Either way, it can be painful.

4.   Ignoring or avoiding the short-term pain that is necessary for us to achieve something important can eventually lead to disappointment. Few achievements come without a price. Although we can gratify many of our needs by getting what we want, that success comes with a price tag on which are written the effort, delay of gratification and sacrifice required. In choosing short-term satisfaction or avoiding immediate pain, we can be self-programming for long-term suffering. When we don't lay down the foundations for success through the patient accumulation of skill or knowledge, we can end up with 'wants' that are inaccessible to us.

5.   The last and most pernicious of these precursors of discontent is avoidance motivation. Rather that expending our energy and attention on pursuing need-satisfaction by closing *the Gap*, we can become focused on avoiding pain. It can seem quite natural to do this when our perceptual system is flooded with images and feelings associated with difficult or traumatic events that we have experienced. We can understand that the mind would like to 'undo' these painful past experiences. However, time-travelling is not an option accessible to the brain. What happened, happened. It's in our memory banks, and the normal activity of the brain and mind can't take it away.

Of course, there are other precursors of misery, other ways in which external circumstances can disrupt the activity of our internal control

---

[1] Developing an external 'locus of control' is often learned early in life. If the adults who guided our formative years offered us only conditional love, then we can develop the habit of thinking that the approval or consent of other people is a condition of our own well-being.

Choosing Misery

system. All of them leave us in the same situation: with a tenacious and painful *Gap* between the real and the ideal in our own mind.

The Gap and the associated distress are inside our own mind, but the related people and events are external. The normal activity of the brain - the generation of a behaviour that can narrow *the Gap* - is frustrated. It's a divide that we cannot figure out how to close. More distressing still is that, like everything the brain does, the suffering becomes automated. The brain naturally turns the thoughts and behaviours associated with our ill-being into habits: into customary dispositions. Synaptic connections are wired into place that sustain our accumulated miseries.

The Adventures of the Creative Brain

Sometimes the choices that lead to unhappiness are made consciously; often they are not. When circumstances are challenging, we do our best to establish some measure of control, either by making a deliberate choice or by following a pathway offered by the habit brain. Either way, the resulting behaviour may help us, but sometimes it does not. For example, responding to external events with grief can be an appropriate behaviour, deliberately chosen to ameliorate recovery. At other times it may be a failure to exercise self-discipline. It was natural for Queen Victoria to grieve for her dead husband, Prince Albert. It may have been self-indulgent of her to wear mourning clothes and adopt the trappings of misery for the remainder of her long life.

Our neural networks - the massive labyrinth of connected cells that we call our brain - are always trying to look after us by finding ways to satisfy our needs and minimise *the Gap* between real and ideal. Mostly they succeed without needing to be too creative; our brain simply modifies or re-directs our previously-learned behaviours.

We all have a huge repertoire of these learned and customary habits - a storehouse of thoughts and actions, feelings and body states which we can call upon to close *the Gap*. In most situations, by adjusting and adapting these behaviours we can lessen our discontent and bring our lives back into balance.

Sometimes, however, our learned pathways to satisfaction fail us. Events around us combine with our imperfect internal processing to complicate rather than improve our lives. Our habituated responses to people and events suddenly don't seem to be helping us deal with them. We grow increasingly frustrated and discontented. *The Gap* between what we want and how things are becomes intrusive and unpleasant. Responding to this frustration, this sense that: 'this is not working', our habit brain activity can be replaced by an unusually erratic series of intrepid synaptic connections.

When this happens, our brain sets off on an adventure. When the existing patterns of brain cell connections are not closing *the Gap*; when the neurons that are habitually 'wired together'[2] don't assuage our discontent, new brain connections are explored. The search for soothing synaptic pathways bounces around like an errant ping-pong ball. New behaviours are attempted. In its search for relief from the strong error signal that our mental processes are emitting, the brain becomes really creative. And our creative brain is not bound by morality, logic, or sanity. It is fallible and imprudent. When it embarks on the search for novel ways to close the burgeoning *Gap*, it throws up all sorts of haphazard options.

In the main, our awareness censors the extreme options. Consciousness helps us manage and control the random possibilities suggested by our searching brain. We don't usually try to dominate our friends and regulate their behaviours; we refrain from punching the irritating colleague on the nose or tell him what we really think. Although the impulse to do so flits through our mind, we don't usually act on our impulses. We don't abandon ourselves to feelings of hopelessness or helplessness, we resist the temptation to abscond from reality, we avoid descending into a fugue

---

[2] Hebbes Law explains that once an electro-chemical connection has been established between two neurons, it increases the chance that it will be repeated and habituated: 'Neurons that fire together wire together.'

Choosing Misery

of depression or delusion. In extremis, however, the inner censor steps back and lets our creative behavioural system have its way.

When our discontent persists, unrelieved by the solutions offered by either our conscious mind or our habit brain, options that may seem to offer greater control can randomly present themselves. When we grow angry at the way life is going, the brain can opt for depression rather than rage. Pushing down our anger dulls its pain, even though the dispiriting consequence is itself unpleasant. When we perceive our reality as inhospitable or hostile, opting for fantasy or imagining a conspiracy can conjure up more invigorating scenarios that cut us off from the threatening world. When danger seems pervasive to us, the brain may embrace chronic anxiety as a shield.

Despite its effects, our creative brain is always purposeful, although its purpose is often hidden from us when we drift from the anchor of 'normal' and effective thought. Whatever its specific nature, psychological distress is confusing and confronting. Our creative brain may be trying to help us, but its choices seem more like interference than assistance.

In these circumstances, misery can seem to have us in its relentless grip. Our well-being is replaced by ill-being. Commonly, we feel helpless and confused by our own creative thoughts, physiology, emotions, or actions. Paradoxically, we don't 'choose' this state, but our choices may lead us there.

The relentless search for new synaptic pathways by the unconscious and reckless brain too easily leads the mind into the dark caverns of despair.

Maladies of the Mind

When these conditions persist, it has become commonplace to give them names and treat them as illnesses of the mind. By labelling them with names such as anxiety disorders, neuroses, depression or even psychoses, we are easily persuaded that they are sicknesses that are similar to physical ailments which need to be treated by medication, or by some kind of therapy. When we give our ill-being these labels, it suggests to us that we have acquired something like a virus, or that we have a genetic weakness, and that we can only recover with the aid of a doctor, therapist, or by treatment with powerful drugs. This medical approach to psychology tempts us to surrender to impotence while we wait to be healed. It seems to exclude the possibility that we can help ourselves.

However, as vulnerable as we feel at these times, we are never completely helpless. *The Gap* that is generating our suffering is in our heads. There are things we can do for ourselves: attitudes we can adopt and behaviours we can choose to retrieve control of our thinking and of our lives.

Let me be clear: I am not advocating that support be shunned in these circumstances. If medication or therapy will aid our recovery, we should call on them. Common sense indicates that there is merit in any practices that aid a sufferer to overcome the sadness and painful thoughts that are impediments to their well-being.

What I am convinced of, however, is that a sense of helplessness (when coupled with these unhappy thoughts) makes things worse. Waiting to be 'healed' does not help us. The unhappy states that are described as mental illnesses are in some respects an 'inside job'.[3] Although the symptoms are real and painful, because their origin can often be the activity of our own brain the remedy always includes the management of our own mind in order to challenge the sense that we are helpless.

Sometimes when I speak or write these things, I can be misunderstood. So, let me clarify this again. I am in no way denying the reality of the pain someone might be experiencing when they are burdened by

---

[3] Dr. William Glasser believed that mental illnesses are amenable to relief through our own agency (perhaps with the aid of therapy) unless there is actual physical damage to the brain.

Choosing Misery

unhappy thinking or daunted by distressing perceptions. The pain is real. By emphasising the role that our own choices may have played in our present distress, I am not trivialising the consequences of this real suffering and its debilitating effects. The unhappiness and misery that are felt in this predicament are not 'made-up' pain - they are distressingly real. That some of them may originate from our own choices does not make them less real. However, knowing the origin of the pain - understanding that it comes from the inside and not the outside - is paradoxically empowering. It means that we have some control. If creative brain activity led to the distress we feel, then it follows that we can be liberated from it by different thinking.

What we **Can** do for Ourselves!

When the brain is not physically damaged, psychological approaches to the 'cure' of behaviours that are not helping us are commonly of 4 types.[4] Whether the behaviours are decorated with a label or not, these interventions (or some combination of them) are the usual remedies that will help us make the transition from painful thoughts and actions towards those that will support our well-being. We can:

• Focus on challenging or modifying our painful perceptions of our present circumstances. Becoming mindfully and objectively critical of our perceptions can remind us that they are inevitably distorted to some extent, and that unhelpful interpretations, fears, and negative predictions are self-created and can be changed. When our map of reality is not helpful, we can update the map.

• Accept the traumatic and distressing events that have occurred in order to move on from them. We cannot change the past, but its effects need not be permanent or predictive. Accepting what has happened, knowing that we cannot change the past, can be the encouragement we need to adopt future-focused thinking. What has happened can't be

---

[4] This somewhat simplifies the range of potential interventions, but it remains true that these four approaches encompass the majority of the mainstream strategies used by cognitive psychologists.

changed, but past events need not prevent us from making new choices and selecting more helpful actions for the future. We can adopt the A.C.T. approach (see Chapter Eight).

- Recognise that unattainable, unreasonable, or unsatisfying goals keep *the Gap* wide and can lead to unnecessary pain. Specifically, when our wants are tied to events that we can't influence, or to people whom we can't control, we are vulnerable to discontent. Wishing things were ideal does not help us to make them so. Aiming for more attainable quality pictures helps us. There will always be a divide between the real and the ideal, but *the Gap* can be managed when realistic and beneficial wants and goals are chosen.

- Choose and practise new behaviours that will enhance our self-management and confidence in ourselves. As humans, we acquire and learn patterns of behaviour (actions, thoughts, emotions, and physiology) that we hope will close *the Gap*. When they don't narrow *the Gap*, we can learn to choose and practise new behaviours. When what we are doing is not working in the interests of our well-being and resilience, it makes sense to choose to do something different.

What I am emphasising with this list of options is the capacity we all have to adopt any of these measures for ourselves. In all these cases, the essential ingredient in recovery is the activation of our own resolve. A therapist may help us face our circumstances and assist us in making new choices. Medication may temporarily dull our pain enough for us to adopt the determination needed to move beyond our present sense of ill-being. Regardless of the interventions offered to help us, if we are to take control of our life our **own will** is central to it.

Most psychology professionals will tell us the same thing: the restoration of wellness requires us to will it. There is no surgery that can reach inside us to adjust our brain or mind. Whatever our mental pain, we have to want to improve things: to live well rather than simply endure; to move beyond the grip of our own distress; to be fierce in our desire for wellness. To wrestle out of the grip of the inhibiting *Gap* requires the determination to thrive.

Choosing Misery

Misery is the antithesis of wellness. It's incongruous that a whole chapter on misery has occupied a book about choosing to thrive! There is no escaping, though, that discontent is a common feature of the human condition. It is a wrong turning, a raucous siren, a bright red flag that tell us that we need to pay attention to the ways in which we are managing our mind. When we surrender to the paralysis of misery, it's easy to do so heedlessly, to relinquish control without noticing. The brain can make a habit from any behaviour, whether it is good for us or not.

Paradoxically, it is at times like these - the occasions when we feel most helpless - that misery can help us, *if* we pay attention. Unhappiness signals to our mind that things are not working. It highlights the importance of making the effort to manage ourselves, to mind the ways in which we are addressing our *Gaps*.

Whether we do this by re-interpreting our harmful perceptions; by accepting that we cannot change historical trauma; by choosing and pursuing attainable wants; or by trying new and more helpful behaviours, we have the tools to manage ourselves towards increased wellness. Knowing what our brain is doing to us in its unsuccessful or inappropriate attempts to help us provides the opportunity for us to take back control.

Our brain is designed to serve us. Sometimes it errs. At such times, our reflective mind can help us by putting the brakes on our creative brain and pushing it firmly in a more helpful direction.

Sixteen

The Challenge of Emotions

Can we choose what we feel?

With everything that brain science has discovered in recent years, we may be in a position to replace Descartes's[1] aphorism: "I think, therefore I am" with the neurobiological insight: 'I feel, therefore I think'!

Emotions, flowing from the energy created by the brain's activity, lead to the emergence of consciousness. Both conceptually and in practice, there is a real sense in which feelings precede thought. Feelings are our 'first responders' to any situation. As such they can be difficult to manage.

In ordinary discourse we rarely differentiate between feelings and emotions - we refer to them as if they are the same phenomena. However, from the neurobiological perspective they are different. Emotions are non-conscious aspects of the activity of the brain. Feelings are our conscious

---

[1] Rene Descartes, the 17th Century philosopher and mathematician, searched for proof of his own existence and concluded that because he could think he must exist.

The Challenge of Emotions

awareness of emotion[2]: they are our inner perception of the emotional brain in action. Emotions are generated by brain sensations. Feelings are our awareness of these sensations.

In the pages of this chapter, I will maintain this distinction, associating emotions with activity in the multiple synaptic connections of the brain, and feelings with our conscious awareness of these emotions. However, in practice, the distinction is inevitably blurred - unconscious emotion is made conscious through feeling. Mood is the extension of feelings over time.

Emotions are good for us. Even emotions that are experienced as pain play a part in keeping us safe and sane:
- Emotions are designed to support our survival, early warning signals that tell us how we are going. Ignoring or suppressing emotion can harm us, increasing our stress and leading to problems with memory and self-concept.
- Feelings enable us to add the vividness and passion that enrich (but sometimes muddle) our lives.
- Emotion is crucial for learning: it activates the feelings of delight that accompany moments of insight and helps us with memory and understanding.

We are creatures of emotion anyway. Nothing can change that. Because we have a well-developed set of middle brain structures, we share our emotional nature with all mammals. As the mammalian brain evolved from the primitive old brain (the reptilian brain), it created our capacity to make changes in the body to help us survive. It doesn't matter that, for most of us, survival is now as much social as it is physical.[3] The emotional

---

[2] I have chosen to make this distinction knowing that it is controversial. Two of the most distinguished scholars in this area, Anthony Damasio and Joseph Ledoux, actively debate the role of consciousness in both emotions and feelings.

[3] David Rock: NeuroLeadership Journal #1, 2008. Rock states that we have social needs for Status, Certainty, Autonomy, Relatedness and Fairness which we strive to satisfy in order to survive in a social world.

brain is ever-present and doing its job, producing in our body hormones that excite or depress our physiology. Emotions respond to our perceptions, preparing us for whatever we notice or anticipate.

In humans, the emotions have two main functions: to give us information, and to energise our motivation when responding to challenges.[4] Feelings tell us how we are going in the peaks and troughs of life. They also help us to respond more fervently to our efforts to close *the Gap* between the real and the ideal. Our feelings also inject urgency into our efforts to avoid threat and hurt.

Because our feelings add intensity to our lives, we often need to manage them. The passions designed to support our survival can sometimes threaten rather than aid our well-being - unless we learn how to limit and control them. In particular, when we experience 'negative' emotions like anger and fear, anxiety, or sadness, too much emotion tends to hinder rather than help us.

Whenever our primitive brain senses danger, it sends urgent panicky messages to the amygdalae – the trigger of our emotional brain. This pair of almond-shaped organs located in the limbic brain is the key to the control of our emotions. To complicate this, it seems that the amygdalae have memory of their own: they instantly recall past instances of fear and trauma and send 'hurry-up' messages to our body, urging it into defensive or offensive action to counter the perception of danger.

We do have some conscious control, but it is weak. There are synaptic connections between the amygdalae and the prefrontal cortex (the brain's control centre), but the neural links going from the amygdalae to the frontal brain appear to be more robust than those going the other way. The result is that feeling often overwhelms thinking. As a result, calming

---

[4] Carroll E. Izzard: The Psychology of Emotions, 1991 - "Emotions are motivational and informational...critical for adaptive responses to immediate challenges to survival or wellbeing."

The Challenge of Emotions

ourselves when we are feeling agitated by the activity of the emotional brain is not easy. It requires us to know what is going on, through our understanding of how the brain works, and then learning and practising self-calming activities.

Feelings – the Management of Internal Perception

If we remember that energy emanating from the activity of the brain is *felt* by us as consciousness, then clearly the 'feeling' aspect of internal perception is critically important. We are always feeling something. Even when our emotions are not being identified in our conscious awareness, they are ever-present. Much of the time this feeling is almost neutral, a kind of background noise to our conscious activity.

At other times, the energy driving these sensations becomes significant enough to loom large in our awareness: sense energy from the brain and body with cognition attached to it. When we are old enough to use regular language to navigate our inner world, we develop the capacity to give a name to the emotion we are feeling. This naming can be very general, such as: 'I feel a bit down today', or quite specific as in: 'I am anxious about my safety' or 'I am excited by the opportunity to try something new'.

The way we name an emotion is important. It is a step towards self-control: the ability to attend to our emotions and calibrate them - to dial them up when we need energy; to self-calm when we need to be composed. As we will see, naming our emotions is one way of regulating them. Just naming an emotion is calming. Whether we name them as negative (sad, fearful, concerned, worried) or as positive (pleased, content, thrilled), giving a name to a feeling is powerful. What we name we can manage – we might call it **'taming by naming'**!

There is a second aspect to 'taming by naming' that is essential to emotional self-control. If we describe an emotion as if it is something that happens to us, the embedded presupposition can lead to a sense of helplessness. Yet the feelings and associated thinking that enter our awareness arise within us. They can't come from outside us. They are self-generated by our brain and, as we will see, they are a behaviour through which we attempt to narrow *the Gap*. Because our feelings are behaviours, they are **verbs**. They are what we do - not something that happens to us.

Talking to ourselves about our emotions in a way that accepts ownership of our feelings helps us to remain in control. They may seem to happen to us, to 'come over us' from outside, but they do not! Emotion is created within us. Even though the actions of the amygdalae are generated in the unconscious, there are ways in which we can manage them by accepting ownership. Asking ourselves: "Why am I doing this?" has a sedative effect when it replaces: "Why is this happening to me?".

Feeling is a behaviour!

As well as being an aspect of our inner perception - a kind of input from within - feeling is also one of the components of our behavioural system; one of the outputs of brain process and mental activity. As you will recall from Chapter Thirteen, we are constantly choosing behaviours that we believe will narrow *the Gap* between what we want and what we are currently perceiving. Every one of these behaviours has four elements: thinking, doing (action), feeling, and a body state or physiology.

These four parts of our behaving can't work independently - they are all aligned with each other. When we have unhappy ***thoughts***, we ***feel*** sad, our ***actions*** tend to be hesitant, our ***physiology*** is despondent. It's impossible to have a happy thought and a sad feeling at the same time; or to feel elated and not show it in our energised actions and physiology. As Dr William Glasser[5] described it, all our behaviour is 'total'. Each of the four outputs of our behavioural system is linked to the others.

The totality of behaviour is helpful when we want to manage our emotions. We can't easily control emotion directly by consciously

---

[5] Dr William Glasser: 'Choice Theory – a New Psychology of Personal Freedom' 1998.

The Challenge of Emotions

'choosing' to have a different emotion. Feelings can't usually be calmed by an act of will. However, if we change our thoughts or our actions, then a change in emotions will accompany these.

As explained in Chapter Twelve, Glasser described total behaviour as being like the wheels of a car. The front wheels of action and thought are the wheels that steer the car. If we want to change direction with them, we can act or think differently and take the 'back wheels' with us.

Changing our emotion or the associated physiology is therefore a two-step process. If we can change the actions and thoughts associated with an unwanted feeling, the feeling will change. I am not suggesting that this is as easy to do as it is to write about, but it is yet another way in which we can manage our emotions and choose total behaviours that help rather than hinder us: **'managing by thinking and doing'**.

Feelings are Linked to Perceptions

A third aspect of feelings to which we can pay attention is their association with perception - the way in which we interpret the external world.

Let me emphasise: it's not the people or events in the world which generate our feelings but our internal interpretation of the external world. When we take in sensory information from the world around us, we process it and use our remembered knowledge and our beliefs and values to give it a mental label. When our experience of events, people or circumstances is satisfying, the neurological connections in our brain connect the event with feelings of pleasure. This connection is often so strong that when we notice something in our external world which was previously associated with strong pleasure, our brain takes a shortcut and we feel pleasure from the sight or sound, taste or touch that was part of the experience. In NLP[6] this is described as an 'anchor'.

Anchoring can be very useful. It's the way in which the brain efficiently connects a behaviour with specific circumstances so that we automatically respond to the people and events around us without having to think it through. I automatically smile when I see a familiar face, even before I have remembered who they are or where I know them from. Less happily, I feel panic when I hear running footsteps behind me in a dark street, long before I have had time to decide whether there is any actual danger.

While an anchor to a positive feeling is rarely problematic, having an anchor to negative events *can* be - especially if it leaves us sensitive to noticing every hint of potential harm or discomfort around us. The ever-vigilant amygdalae are highly-tuned to connect our present perception with past trauma or threat. When there is even a whiff of these, the amygdalae activate the brain's function to protect and preserve. In protecting us, it can sometimes do its job too well!

Responses that were built into our genes to protect us from sabre-toothed tigers do not serve us well when they initiate hostility towards a colleague, or anxiety about an event where we need to be at our best.

Because paying attention is a thinking behaviour, not an emotion, we can intentionally direct our perceptions. Noticing that what we are paying attention to is anchored to an *unhelpful* emotion, we can choose to focus on some other aspect of our perceived experience. If a past experience of public speaking has ended badly (because I stumbled over my words and felt foolish and inadequate), then I might import these anchored feelings to every future invitation to speak in front of a group. Alternatively, I can attend to how well I know my subject, how different this new situation is, how confident I am in other situations, or how well-prepared I am on this

---

[6] NLP (Neuro-Linguistic-Programming) is a methodology that explores the connections between mental activity, language and behaviour. NLP is the source of many useful strategies for managing the mind.

The Challenge of Emotions

different occasion. We might call this way of managing emotion **'managing by attending'** – a form of mindfulness.

We have a choice here. As we prepare for an important event, we can recall the times that we have been successful in the past; or we can hinder our performance by focusing our thinking on our past failures. When we need to concentrate on an important but complex task, we can dwell on the difficulty of the work, or alternatively notice the steady progress being made. Attending to the positive rather than the negative changes the associated emotions.

In summary: we can make choices that help us to manage our emotions. Even though we cannot change an emotion directly by an act of will, we can manage it indirectly through our thoughts and actions and by the way in which we focus our attention.

Let's finish this chapter by looking in detail at two ways in which we can increase our emotional control:
1. By learning to calibrate our feelings.
2. Through activating our curiosity.

Adjusting our Emotions

Strong emotion is hard to shake off. When we are 'absolutely incensed' by the thoughtless action of another person, the way we are naming our feelings has a lot to do with the intensity and influence of the sensations that are generated in our body. There is a bond between language, emotion, and physiology. When one changes, so do the others.

Try this exercise: think of a person or event that you have recently associated with annoyance. As you recall the event that led to your feelings of displeasure, change the language that you use in describing what happened. Talk to yourself in your head as you do this. Start from "It was annoying" and then escalate the degree of emotion to "It left me so angry" to "He was deliberately infuriating" and then to "He left me incandescent with rage". Notice what is happening in your body as you change the way you name your feelings. The words you use create greater tension and discomfort in your body as they escalate, especially if you identify the **cause** of the feelings as another person or event. We talk to ourselves constantly. This kind of self-talk is not helpful.

Now take your thoughts in the opposite direction. Once again think about the event that you described to yourself as 'annoying' and change your description to "I became a little bit frustrated" or "I felt a bit cross" or "I was slightly miffed" or "I chose negative thoughts".

Notice that I was suggesting that you change two things – and both are important:
1. Choose words that communicate a different level of intensity.
2. As the intensity of the feeling diminishes, use words that take ownership of the feeling.

I call this 'emotional calibration': the adjustment of the instrument of emotion by activating the distinctions between the words we use. Emotional calibration is the ability to dial our emotions up or down by using the metacognitive power of mind.

What is often named 'emotional intelligence' is closely tied to our ability to adjust our emotions purposefully in our interaction with other people.

Extending our emotional vocabulary helps us to calibrate effectively. By using a wider range of words to describe our feelings, it is much easier to change our naming of an emotion. If we have very few words to use in naming anger (perhaps just 'mad', 'in a rage', 'furious') then our capacity to change the intensity of emotions is limited. As we increase our emotional vocabulary, it then becomes less effortful to manage our feelings.

When we can call on an extensive vocabulary of emotional words related to anger, such as: furious, enraged, irate, cross, indignant, irritated, piqued, aggrieved, riled, frustrated, confronted, displeased, upset,

The Challenge of Emotions

troubled, concerned, perturbed, unsettled, disconcerted, peeved, miffed, uneasy, uptight, flustered …… then we have the potential for greater control. With more emotional settings to choose from on the dial[7] we have greater emotional flexibility.

The other important step is to use language that claims ownership of our feelings. Talking and thinking about our feelings as verbs (referring to what we do) provides us with leverage. We are always the source of what we feel. Just because feeling sensations are not easily amenable to cognitive control does not mean that we can't manage them. It means that doing so takes effort and practice.

Curiosity is kind to us

Any of the bundles of neural collections that automate our feelings can either be well adapted or poorly constructed for their task. Sadly, we don't always adopt emotional behaviours that are good for us! When an unhelpful behaviour schema is learned and automated, we can tend to self-sabotage. Emotional pain is connected to a situation. The emotions of frustration and discouragement swamp our system, leading to psychological dysfunction – unhelpful habits of thought and behaviour. To counter this, it is helpful to activate an emotion that is always present in our mind. We can be curious!

The emotion of 'interest' is almost always present when a healthy mind is functioning normally. Being interested or curious is the co-driver of our central motivation: the urge to detect and close a *Gap* between whatever is happening and our ideal. With curiosity, we look for a way to close *the*

---

[7] There is increasing evidence that the 'names' we give to emotions are highly individual descriptions - personal markers on the 'continuum of arousal' (Lisa Feldman Barrett: 'How Emotions Are Made', 2018). Our inner perceptions of emotions are affected by culture and personal history. However, the uniqueness of our emotions and the very personal way they are created are linked to our ability to use language signals to manage the degrees of arousal involved.

Gap and not to fear it. As long as we are engaged in working out how to narrow *the Gap*, our sense of well-being is maintained.

Being interested, curious, or puzzled takes us forward to create new schemas and to foster our adaptation to the changing world. We can use this ever-present emotion to manage whatever confronts us. Whenever we react to actions or events that we experience as confronting, we do have the option of curiosity.

Becoming curious - instead of responding with a more primitive emotional response - has to be learned. The impulse to fight or flee is not easy to override unless we have a well-practised, habituated behaviour to call upon. However, we can learn to activate curiosity and make it our default habit. If we start small and deliberately wonder 'why?' when we encounter behaviours by others that we don't understand, we can lay down the foundations for a new default setting.

Asking ourselves *why* something is happening takes our thinking into a more objective space - to the observer mode of thinking. In this space, some emotion may still be present, but it will be less intrusive. We will still feel the automatic change in physiology that is our first sign of the disturbance of the 'unknown' or 'not understood'. However, linking this feeling to a chain of synaptic connections that already exist - our propensity to feel interested - enables us to transcend the primitive brain response – at least to some extent!

That qualification is important. We don't want to extinguish the survival response – indeed, we can't anyway. And the survival instinct serves us well. No amount of self-calming will help us when we are in the jaws of a metaphorical sabre-toothed tiger!

Emotional Control

Emotional control is achievable. The six self-calming practices named in this chapter can help:

1. Taming by naming.

The Challenge of Emotions

2. Identifying ourselves as the source of our emotional behaviours.
3. Managing our thoughts and actions.
4. Paying attention to our perceptions.
5. Calibrating our emotional intensity.
6. Activating curiosity instead of hostility.

However, none of these practices can become customary without mental effort. As we saw in Chapter Four, choosing to change can involve a great deal of mindful effort. The emotions and associated behaviours that we find distressing are entrenched in the brain's activity through wired-in synaptic connections. We can replace them and modify them through these six alternative ways of thinking - but adopting a new set of synaptic switches and learning to prefer them to the unwanted ones takes time and practice.

Accepting that feeling is something we **do** - a behaviour that we create - provides us with the impetus to act differently.

Seventeen

Desirable Doubt

The Freedom of an Open Mind

Certainty is a trap for the unwary mind. Its allure is that it seems to offer the illusion of safety and control. If the world around us were stable and predictable, that illusion might be useful. However, because we live in an ever-changing environment, it can become a threat to our well-being.

Clinging to whatever we feel sure about can appear to bring with it a sense of control. Thinking that we are right provides an illusion of protection in the face of our human fragility. Misled by conviction, it's a temptation to ignore the way that inflexibility of thought is a barrier to the ability to solve problems. It is adaptability, not certainty, that helps us to thrive. Disciplining ourselves to live with incertitude through the exercise of an open mind is what serves us.

The arithmetic of knowledge seems to be a comfort if we take the simplistic view. After all, we can reason: 'The more I know the less I don't know'. That sounds logical. More knowledge, like more money in the bank, might create a hedge against a fickle future.

Desirable Doubt

Except that knowledge is not like that. A better metaphor for the balance between knowledge and ignorance is Einstein's Circle.[1] If we imagine our knowledge as a circle, then everything outside that circle represents what we don't know. As the area of the circle increases, so does its circumference. Thus, the larger the circle of knowledge, the greater the perimeter of our interface with ignorance. This 'geometry of ignorance' humbles us. As knowledge expands, so should our awareness of how much we still have to learn.

It takes a certain amount of courage to face the real mathematics of 'knowing', and the inevitable implication of the vastness of our own nescience. It feels safer to snuggle in the cave of what we **do** know and understand, than to venture into the travails of uncertainty. However, this safety is an illusion.

Not only is certainty a threat to our adaptability, but it also defies both the science of mind and our everyday experience of the variety of human perception. When we believe that we are right - when we are sure that the subject of our conviction is the absolute and certain truth - we are asserting something that is quite unlikely. Insisting that we are right whatever others may think is to claim that our perceptions correspond exactly with something 'true' in the real world.

We do rely on our beliefs. They are perceptions of course, but trusted perceptions. Time and experience have assured us that what we believe provides us with useful information about how things are; about how the world works. However, to believe without our perception being open to review is not so useful.

However strong our reliance on them, our perceptions are inevitably interpretations. Our unique personal conceptions of the 'reality' outside

---

[1] Attributing this to Einstein may well be an urban myth. It has also been attributed to Pascal and various other luminaries. It's an important insight, whoever first drew attention to it. In essence, the more we know, the more we can become aware of what we don't yet know.

ourselves are filtered by what we know and who we are. As explained a few chapters back, the lenses of our mind help us to interpret sense data in order to create a map, an approximation, of the real world. From energy transmitted by objects and events existing outside ourselves, we use our interpretive capacity to plot the landscape of reality. Generally speaking, the maps we make serve us well enough to navigate the actual events and objects, people and places that constitute our environment. In most respects, they will be close enough to the maps created by others for us to co-exist and communicate with them.

Our maps are useful to us so long as they are up to date. We try to construct them so that they share enough correspondence with 'reality' for us to get by - until we encounter a moment or an experience that challenges our representation of the 'real'. When that happens, if our minds are open, if we are dedicated to truth, we upgrade our map.

Unless we are certain that we are right!

The Mind that Closes

The secret to being able to keep our map up to date is an open mind. Accepting new or conflicting information and incorporating it into our prior understanding is learning. Reassessing and revising boundaries and limits is what our brain was designed for. New schemas (arrangements of brain connections) are created when an existing array of synaptic connections is added to or modified. Our ability to create, revise and reorganise our neural connections is the defining characteristic of the most agile and adaptable creature in the world – homo sapiens.

Although it may be central to both our ingenuity (and our well-being), willingness to keep on updating our maps of reality throughout are lives is precious but rare. Making what seems an entirely satisfactory map, and then allowing it to be challenged by a new feature of the ever-shifting circumstances in which we are immersed, is disquieting - but essential if we are going to thrive.

Desirable Doubt

Many people resist updating their maps. They have completed a 'near enough is good enough' depiction of reality by early adulthood. By mid-life, an even greater percentage of people have settled upon the map that they will resolutely depend on. Thenceforth, they will try to avoid noticing any conflict with actuality. But the world around us is no ally of this resistance to novelty. It keeps changing. Consequently, we battle with unwanted perceptions by telling ourselves: 'It should not be like that' as though our 'should-ing' can buttress us against the tides of change.

Truths we had taken for granted are always being challenged. Whether the novel problems we face come from science or culture, the shifting of the tectonic plates or the spread of new diseases, uncertainty frames the context of our lives. Who predicted that so many of the 'normalities' we took for granted would be threatened by Covid-19? How many people anticipated that fundamental economic principles that we had accepted would be quickly abandoned in the face of widespread disease: that not only lives but also livelihoods would be so easily threatened?

The problem is that unwillingness to keep our maps up to date leaves us stuck in the world of make-believe and powerless to adapt. For intrigued spectators, the spectacular polarity of American political opinion in recent years is an illustration of how widely perception can be stretched to fit the truths we want to hear. Each side is so convinced of their rightness that nothing is commonly regarded as reliable evidence. One side's evidence is the other's conspiracy! The consequence is mulish intransigence. When both sides feel certain, who is going to move?

Although we have known for decades the way in which perception works, we can still be surprised by the most egregious examples of its ability to divide. Truly, we do see the world as we create it, not as it is. Our acquired preferences, assumptions, prejudices and preconceptions distort the way we see things, eschew anything we do not care to know, and make astonishing connections between unconnected ideas.

Feeling that we are right, despite the overwhelming evidence that it's very easy to be wrong, both divides and disables us. We make adversaries of each other because of our reluctance to consider the ideas of others and work together. And when both our conceptions of the ideal and our perceptions of the real are dislocated from the shifting currents of external evidence, the space between the two may seem increasingly unbridgeable.

The Attraction of Feeling 'Right'

'I am right, and you are wrong' has a calamitous history. It's a history as long as the human race; a deplorable trail of conflict and contention that damages relationships and has inaugurated innumerable wars. Religious institutions and political enemies feed on its energies. Academic bigotries, often based on ambiguous research or divisive opinions, stretch the credibility of experts. As a person who strives to keep his own maps up to date, I cringe whenever I hear the phrase 'the science is settled' from one side or another in any debate.

For those of us who pay attention to how our brains learn and how our minds adapt and change on the basis of new data, unwillingness to doubt is confronting. Yet, being both the operator and observer of my own brain in action, I do understand why the feeling that we are right is so enticing. *Feeling* that 'we know something' feels good!

As we understand it, the brain learns by creating new synaptic bridges between what we already know and new information we receive. Creating the early connections between the new and the established involves building a new bridge. Earlier, I compared it to trusting a fragile thread until, through repeated use, it becomes a firm connection. When the tenuous connection between neurons is nourished by repetitive crossing of the synaptic gap, a more enduring connection is established. By firing together, the neurons become wired together.[2]

In order to encourage that first feeble step in the process that we call learning, the brain encourages us with tiny injections of dopamine into

---

[2] Hebbes law: Neurons that fire together, wire together.

Desirable Doubt

our brain. Dopamine is a neurotransmitter: it facilitates the connections between neurons. The infusion of dopamine also feels good. It's a self-created internal pleasure 'drug' on which the human organism thrives. When we get that first flash of 'maybe' - that instant on the threshold of insight - the thrill of dopamine urges us on. When that initial feeling of internal arousal is further rewarded by a sense of new knowledge or profound understanding, dopamine rewards us again. The feeling of knowing, of intense clarity, is euphoric, personally validating and deeply gratifying. **And it's a feeling**!

If we accept the hypothesis that all behaviour is a composition of thought and action, feeling and bodily state, then it's more than likely that 'thinking we are right' owes more to sensation than to cognition. We can't have a thought that is disconnected from feeling. When we feel we are right, we identify that certainty with the cognitive element of total behaviour. However, as Robert Burton[3] argues, the sense of being right is derived from the feeling component of the behaviour, not from the correspondence of our thought with any objective reality. Indeed, Burton explains convincingly that 'objectivity' is probably impossible for the human mind, susceptible as it is to the bias of past experience and present presupposition.

Why does certainty persist?

A brief feeling of 'knowing' might then be useful to us, but why does it persist into a settled state? Why does the 'feeling of certainty' have an extended existence beyond the 'aha!' moment? As far as I know, the explanation for this is not clear. However, it seems possible that the dopamine-fuelled pleasure that is generated by the sensation that we are 'right' is extended in time by the related gratification of other needs. Because we have genetic needs to be powerful, influential and in control, we employ our certainty in the service of these needs. All need-satisfying

---

[3] Robert Burton: 'On Being Certain. Believing That You Are Right Even When You Are Wrong', 2008.

behaviours attract dopamine rewards. When the dopamine reward of 'knowing' is linked to a feeling of power, certainty is attractive.

It is probably the attraction of the feeling that we are the exclusive keepers of 'rightness' that pits religious beliefs into conflict with each other. In spite of having remarkably similar origins and the common adoption of 'the Golden Rule'[4], the major religions, and the sectarian divides within those religions, are usually focused on their differences, not their similarities. This tendency to exclude and to deride those who do not share exactly similar beliefs is the antithesis of the compassion that most religions preach.

Of course, this tendency is not the exclusive domain of religious institutions. Political parties, tribes and nations also draw on the energy fuelled by both prejudice and a sense of superiority.

The 'Knowing' that Embraces Doubt.

The irony of writing a book about how I perceive the brain and mind while mistrusting certainty is not lost on me. I am presenting my own inevitably incomplete understanding as 'true', even while I promote the value of doubt! In presenting my view of the working of the brain and mind and suggesting that applying this knowledge is helpful for our well-being and resilience, I am putting forward a perception that I believe to be useful. And yet I have just confessed that my belief that these ideas are both correct and useful is based on feeling rather than objective truth.

I don't think that this is entirely a contradiction. The history of ideas, the methodology of science and the exploration of the physical and psychological worlds, are advanced by those who offer their best understanding of 'truth' as an invitation for it to be corrected. I would

---

[4] 'The Golden Rule' is the principle of treating others as one would like to be treated. It is a maxim that is found in most religions and cultures.

Desirable Doubt

argue that my writing is useful precisely because it is influenced by the **search** for meaning and truth. Asserting that I am 'right' is no part of it. I think of my present state of understanding as a stage in my own learning - one that might be useful to others. I am fairly sure that there is an important difference!

When we are genuinely searching for 'truth', we are always open to doubt. Even as I advocate for an understanding of mind that will help us manage ourselves, I am resigned to the inevitability of different information. In exploring and sharing the present limits of my own understanding, I am aware of the vast empire of my own ignorance. By sharing what I know, or at least what I *feel* I know, I am moving deliberately towards the expansion of my own understanding.

Within the limits of my learning and expression, I choose to communicate my deeply held belief that we can mind *the Gap* between the ideal and the real with greater contentment if we understand the capabilities of our own brain, the limitations of our mind. If it turns out that I am mistaken in either detail or entirety, I will be encouraged to seek more learning and a deeper sense of meaning.

Ignorance is not to be feared. It allows us to open ourselves to learning.

As long as we know that we have something to learn - that the elusive premium of truth lies beyond us (but is worth reaching for) - we will strive and thrive. As humans, it is in extending our limits that we flourish. As Alfred North Whitehead[5] wrote: "Not ignorance, but ignorance of our ignorance is the death of knowledge."

Certainty closes the boundaries of exploration. Doubt liberates us to thrive.

---

[5] Alfred North Whitehead was an English philosopher and mathematician who was the founder of 'Process Philosophy'. He believed that reality consists of 'states' rather than objects.

Section 5: Thriving in the Gap

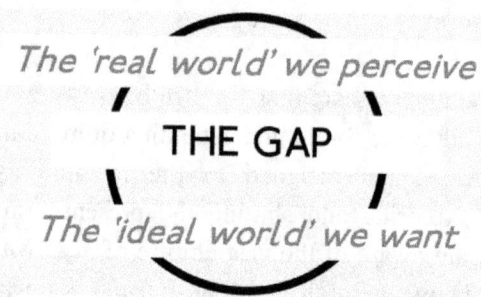

"We are our choices."

Jean-Paul Sartre

"In the simplest terms, what underpins 'thriving' is feeling good about life and yourself and being good at something."

Dr Daniel Brown

"A joyful life is an individual creation that cannot be copied from a recipe."
Mihalyi Csikszentmihalyi

Is What I am Doing helping me?

Eighteen

Is what I am Doing Helping me?

The Legacy of Dr William Glasser

In 1965, a then little-known psychiatrist working in a Californian Correctional Facility for young women[1] wrote a book that ushered a new approach to mental health onto the public stage.[2]

Psychiatry had long been the province of those working to treat or heal 'mental illness.' Its practices included treatments that were usually lengthy, often ineffective, and sometimes downright cruel. With the publication of 'Reality Therapy', Dr. William Glasser drew attention to a different purpose for psychiatry: the quest for mental health. He developed and taught practices that showed individuals how to take responsibility for their own well-being and happiness.

Although many of the people with whom he worked in the early years of his practice believed that they were helpless in the face of their

---

[1] The Ventura School for Girls, California, established 1913.
[2] 'Reality Therapy – a new Approach to Psychiatry' 1965.

predicaments, Glasser showed them that there were ways for them to change their thoughts and actions in order to lead satisfying lives.

Nowadays, when I introduce Dr. Glasser's ideas to a group, I often describe his practices and his theory[3] as 'the psychology of optimal performance'. They show how a person can manage their own mind in order to thrive.

Glasser's experience as described in his book 'Reality Therapy', and elaborated and refined through his subsequent publications[4], introduced me to many of the themes of this book. Among other radical changes in the practice of psychology, he advanced the proposition that, however difficult and unhappy our lives seem to be, we are never helpless. We can learn how to improve and maintain our own mental health. Although changing ourselves and the direction of our lives is never easy, it is rarely impossible.

The First Step

We can have greater control of our lives if we are prepared to take the first step: to ask ourselves honestly if our present behaviours and our past choices are contributing to our well-being. Are they healing or hurting our current state of mind? Are they making things better or worse? Is *the Gap* between what we want and our perceptions of reality growing less painful or more intrusive?

These seem like such obvious questions. Yet entangled as we are by the fine details of our living, they demand an honesty that is challenging to face. We are the person we have become, shaped by the internal ancestry of our own perceptions and behaviours. We are used to defending our past

---

[3] Glasser practised a counselling process which he named 'Reality Therapy', and which eventually came to be explained by the theory which he called 'Choice Theory'.
[4] Dr. William Glasser was the author of over 20 books.

choices, not questioning them. Asking ourselves whether we have taken some wrong turnings is like abandoning a well-worn and treasured garment that no longer quite fits us.

Although all of us have stepped into this present moment by making decisions that seemed the best option at the time, the choices of the creative brain can steer us to a place that is far from ideal. When we accept the proposition that it is what we have chosen (perhaps inadvertently) and are presently choosing that is not helping us, we can subsequently adopt new behaviours and make changes.

Choices that are intended to protect or even serve us can easily turn out to be unhelpful. Shunning a skill because our first attempts ended in an embarrassing failure can seem rational at the time. Deciding not to pursue a career because it would take too long to gain the required qualification, or, conversely, accepting the offer of a well-paid job in an area that holds no interest for us, are the kinds of choices that may backfire.

Similarly, developing perfectionism in early life is quite common, but can be an eventual source of anguish. Perfecting our work often wins the approval of parents and teachers. The accompanying attention to detail and relentless urge to get things 'absolutely right' brings success. On the downside, this kind of commitment to flawlessness can lead easily to an unhelpful belief: a belief that nothing we do is good enough.

At the time this schema - this pattern of behaviour - develops, it seems to serve us well. People who like things to be perfect present to others as conscientious and internally motivated. However, the inner striving for success (a good thing) can be distorted by such high internal standards that success becomes almost unattainable. Those who have learned to be self-critical in this way can come to view the world around them through the lens of their habit of self-criticism. They consistently undervalue their own achievements and minimise their own talents in comparison with what they perceive to be the accomplishments of others – which are often proportionally over-valued.

The resulting world view is not a happy one! In these circumstances, the inner perception of personal shortcomings compared to the imagined ideal makes it very hard to be contented. For people in this self-created bind, the sense in which they 'choose' unhappiness becomes detached from our normal understanding of choice.

The attitude that creates the pain that they feel is the result of the accumulation of past choices. Attitudes that were adopted to support self-improvement become the rack upon which the tortured present perception of pain is experienced. Choices that were well-intentioned have led into a blind alley of unhappiness.

These habits of mind, forged in the synaptic brain, are pervasive - but don't need to be permanent.

We didn't 'choose' the discontent we now experience – at least not in the sense of a deliberate decision. The young women in the Ventura School did not choose to be imprisoned. It is simply that decisions made in the past translate into habits that then become obstacles to our later preferences. Facing the knowledge that we have acquired self-limiting scripts, or patterns of behaviour that are leading to our own distress, can feel painfully discouraging. To liberate ourselves, we have to push through this pain. What we once chose, we can subsequently reject. We can choose differently, although not without effort and commitment.

Even deep-seated personal traits, such as the habit of defensiveness or a preference for pessimism, can be challenged and changed with effort.

Self-Evaluation – 'Is this working for me?'

Self-evaluation - which pre-supposes that we are internally controlled - was critical to the procedures that Glasser introduced to the young offenders in the Ventura School, and subsequently to millions of people across the globe. What he taught was that everyone is always striving to satisfy their basic needs, and that failure to succeed in this regard leads to

Is What I am Doing helping me?

many of the 'symptoms' that surface in people's behaviour. When our conventional and responsible ways of satisfying our needs are not working, our brain's capacity to invent is deployed.

When we are unhappy and our needs are frustrated, we feel out of control. It seems as if what we are experiencing is somehow imposed upon us from outside ourselves. We blame other people or the events around us for what is happening within us. In the words of the song:

"You think it's easier
To put your finger on the trouble
When the trouble is you.
And you think it's easier
To know your own tricks
Well it's the hardest thing you'll ever do."[5]

Accepting that your troubles are within you is not easy at all! For many people, it **is** close to the hardest mental work they will ever undertake. Acknowledging that it is our own mental processes that are resulting in the blind alleys of our life - often through the way in which we are attempting to close *the Gap* - takes courage. However, if we can ask ourselves the frank and probing questions that recognise that our own choices are inseparable from the pain we are feeling, we are empowered. When we accept that it is our own 'tricks' (our own creative brain activities) that are leading to the pain, and that the trouble is within ourselves, we can begin to assert control. When we know that we can deliberately identify and choose other behaviours - behaviours that can help us to feel better - we have begun to break free from the thrall of our helpless thinking.

The questions: 'What am I doing?' and 'Are my thoughts and actions helping me or hurting me?' are powerful because they are mirrors of the activity of the healthy brain. As human control systems, we are ceaselessly comparing our present circumstances either with the need-satisfying

---

[5] U2 'The Troubles', 2014.

'wants' that motivate us or with the pain and distress that we are trying to avoid.

When our brains are working optimally, they are always occupied by this never-ending search for the best way to close *the Gap* and satisfy our needs. When the brain experiences frustration, it naturally avoids pain – it sets out on a search for a solution. These self-evaluation questions are congruent with the processing of our normal brain activity: 'If what I am doing brings pain, what else can I do?'

Questions such as these bring our normal synaptic searching to our awareness in a way that enables us to accept that our present thinking, acting and emotions are not helping!

Whenever our perceptions are painful to us, we choose behaviours that we hope will improve things. Sometimes we get it wrong. Seeking to avoid pain, we choose behaviours that are different, but which turn out to be no better. In time, these alternatives can be even more painful than the original malaise. The only way we can begin the shift from feeling distressed and discontented to feeling well and happy is to accept that what we are presently doing is not working. *The Gap* is increasing, not diminishing, but like the frog in boiling water we are slow to perceive our worsening situation.[6]

Our awareness that each of us is an internal control system that has created and is prolonging our pain takes helplessness out of the equation. If the mechanisms of past choices got us to this unhappy moment in our lives, then future choices can move us towards a state of contentment or acceptance that will enable us to thrive.

The crux is the willingness to honestly evaluate our own situation. Nobody can do this for us. Someone else may tell us that what we are

---

[6] If a frog is placed in water that is very gradually brought to the boil, it does not perceive its peril until the heat has sapped the strength required for it to jump out of the pan and escape its fate – or so goes the myth!

Is What I am Doing helping me?

doing is not working, but it will avail us nothing if we do not self-evaluate. Our own brain and mind respond to internal prompting, not to the critical opinion of others.

The powerful questions we can ask ourselves are always: 'Is what I am doing helping me?'; 'Are my present thoughts and actions reducing my pain or making it worse?'.

As *the Gap* grows uncomfortably, it is by changing our language that we can nudge our thinking towards the capacity to help ourselves. The language of personal responsibility stands at odds with the language of external control. When we accept that the unhappiness that pervades our thinking can be managed by the way we talk to ourselves, we can begin to ask:

- 'Is what I am thinking and doing helping me to close the space between how I am feeling and how I would like to feel?'
- 'Are my thoughts working to bring me closer to what I want?'
- 'Is thinking that I am helpless making my life better or worse?'

and crucially:

- 'What else can I do?'

When we have taught ourselves to ask these questions honestly, and we subsequently behave congruently with the answers that we give to our own questions, we are occupying the productive life-space where our choices contribute to thriving.

Nineteen

Happiness and 'the Good Life'

Is there a Recipe for 'the Good Life'?

We would all like to live 'the good life', although it's not always clear what that means.

I recently read a one-word definition: 'enough'.

That is succinct but ambiguous. It implies that to live well we have to accumulate: enough money, enough love, or enough fame perhaps. And how much is enough? We would all have different answers. That question takes us in the wrong direction anyway: accumulation implies that well-being comes from outside us, a supposition that is contradicted by the thesis of this book.

The absence of a recipe for good living is the ineluctable consequence of our nature. We are creatures of choice, crafting our own wellness or ill-being from the substance and direction of the life that we manage alone. Not being able to contrive an infallible road to our own happiness, having to work it out through the trials of our own experience, is just another consequence of the way in which we are created as products of our own brain and its receptive mind. Because none of our minds is a clone of any other, we must look *inside* in order to work out how to thrive.

The quest for a single definition or a single formula for a good life is bound to fail for two reasons:
- Firstly, because every attempt at identifying a blueprint for human contentment tends to be confounded by the uniqueness of each human mind; by the manner in which our control system forms itself and creates its own reference points. The result is that no set of precepts or list of behaviours will steer us infallibly towards a common pathway to contentment or personal evolution. All attempts to find a package that will tie 'the road to well-being' with a neat bow inevitably encounter the obstacle of human difference.
- Secondly, because our well-being is inevitably a self-creation. We can't stumble across it - or acquire the elements of a good life by picking them off a 'wellness tree'. We construct our well-being through the way in which we manage our internal control systems, the goals we set ourselves, the capabilities we choose to develop, the resilience we acquire through dealing with difficulties.

Because we are all unique and have different wants, a life in which we learn to thrive is probably more like a distinctive patchwork quilt than a single formula. Well-being is composed from a personal pattern of goals and desires, achievements and pre-dispositions, attitudes and decisions. We have to choose the elements of this melange for ourselves. As always, choosing is how we manage our life. When we are aspiring to thrive, it's helpful to consider the choices that may be the most beneficial to that quest.

The 'Happiness' Element

Do we need to be happy to thrive?

There may be some elements of a life in which we feel that we are flourishing that don't pre-suppose happiness, but a degree of contentment would probably be on most people's list of what it takes to thrive. At least, let's agree that it would be unusual to claim that one is miserable but thriving!

The inconvenience is that happiness is hard to pin down. J.S. Mill[1] famously observed: "The moment we ask ourselves if we are happy, we are not!"

Helpfully, the Positive Psychology movement has attempted to identify some key elements of a happy life. In a succinct but powerful TED talk[2], Martin Seligman suggests that there are three kinds of happiness, or as he put it, three happy lives:
1. A life of pleasure
2. A life of engagement
3. A meaningful life

He implies that each of these may be necessary (and together they may be sufficient) for a good life. I think it may well be more complicated than that, but his framework is a helpful starting place.

The Pleasant Life?

We know that all life is attended by pleasure and pain, in varying degrees. When a genetic need is satisfied, we feel pleasure. When our needs are thwarted or threatened, we experience pain. The 'pleasant life' would presumably be one in which many needs are satisfied.

When Aristotle[3] discussed the nature of 'the good life', he contrasted 'eudaemonia' (the life well-lived) with hedonism, a life of pleasure. He characterised hedonism as self-indulgent, a way of life in which the

---

[1] John Stuart Mill, 19th Century English Philosopher
[2] Martin Seligman, author of 'Flourish', speaking at a TED talk - **TED2004** | February 2004.
[3] Aristotle [384– 322 BCE] was a pupil of Plato and is sometimes regarded as the 'father of western philosophy'. His 'Nichomachean Ethics' was a sustained exploration of the conditions of a good life.

gratification of sensual pleasures is the preoccupation of the human organism. For Aristotle, pursuing 'pleasure', the lust for short-term satisfactions, was not to be confused with the good life. He characterised the good life as eudaemonic, a life in which we come to possess and enjoy what is good **for** us.

The distinction Aristotle drew between what feels good to us and what is good **for us** is helpful. We know the difference: chocolate may taste good, but healthy eating is good for us. Distracting ourselves with virtual entertainment fills the hollow spaces of an isolated life, but it can't compare with the nourishing face-to-face connection of friends and loved ones. Possessing some wealth and the ease it offers may be pleasurable, but being rich and self-indulgent does not guarantee happiness.

That said, we should not write off pleasure. All of us are hooked on it! Responding to feelings of pleasure is an essential feature of how the brain works. The pleasant life alone may not be enough for happiness, but it is surely a key dimension of the human condition. We are certainly motivated to pursue our personal versions of pleasure and avoid what we experience as painful.

In talking about 'the pleasant life', Seligman implies that the pleasure from need-satisfaction contributes most to our happiness when it is both sought and appreciated. I think he is right on two counts:
- Firstly, because our most valued 'ideal' experiences don't just fall into our laps. Accumulating the capabilities and competency that will enable us to become powerful and influential individuals takes time and commitment. Nurturing close relationships with friends and family members requires sustained effort. The pleasures which are most rewarding are often the hardest won.
- Secondly, because we can easily miss the opportunities for happiness if we are not on the look-out for them - and if we don't tune our minds to the enjoyment they bring. Pleasure passes without notice if we don't take time to savour it. Just as important - whether the incidence of need-satisfaction is linked to success, or relationships, the exercise of autonomy, or simply having fun - pleasure is amplified if we are

grateful for it. Gratitude and appreciation are two of the stewards of a happy life.

What I think this means is that pleasure might be one consideration if we want to thrive, but no part of this dimension of well-being is accidental. The pleasures that count towards thriving must be those which are actively pursued, not merely the indulgences that come to us effortlessly if we have plenty of money or power.

Surveys do show that people who are wealthy report that it's easier to access pleasant diversions, and that there are fewer constraints on the ways in which they entertain themselves. However, whether we are rich or poor, most of us discover that it's not the ability to fill the hours of our life that matters, it's how we fill those hours. We can have easy access to everything money can buy, but still feel unhappy. Thriving is more than plentiful incidences of gratification.

It's a predictable feature of the human condition that we often fail to notice our own satisfactions and hanker instead for someone else's (especially someone we believe to have 'more'). As a result, we often hear one version or another of: 'If only I had their life I would be happy.' There is no evidence that this supposition is valid. Knowing that all our thoughts and feelings are individually constructed from the inside helps us to accept that this is a fallacy. We can't have any life but our own, and we can have no idea of what it would be like to live in any other person's 'bag of skin'. What matters is gratifying our needs through the experiences that are 'ideal for us'.

Engaged by *the* Gap

The human experience of striving is instructive. Striving is struggling with a challenge. It may take us closer to the eudaemonic experience than the occurrences of pleasure. It may well be one of our best clues to what it means to thrive.

Happiness and the Good Life

This brings us to the conditions for Seligman's second kind of 'happy': the experience of engagement. It seems that we can be profoundly content and often feel that we are happily thriving when *the Gap* between what we want and what we experience is both preoccupying us and energising us. Becoming immersed in tackling problems is potentially another kind of happiness. We can become engaged in the activity of pursuing quality and find *that* experience so intrinsically satisfying that we shut out everything else. Pursuing a particular goal or solving an interesting problem seems worthwhile for its own sake. Far from being distressed by *the Gap* between what we want and how things are, we can become happily lost in addressing the challenge of narrowing it.

This seems like a very different kind of happiness from the satisfaction of the senses. As Mihaly Csikszentmihalyi[4] writes: "The best moments of our lives are not passive ..... the best moments occur when our mind and body are stretched to their limits in a voluntary effort to achieve something difficult and worthwhile."

Csikszentmihalyi describes this state of focused engagement as 'flow'. When experienced by an athlete or an artist, it is often described as being 'in the zone'. 'Flow' is more than just useful work and invigorating play; it is being so deeply immersed in action or thought that we become engaged in it for its own sake. When we are absorbed in our work, or our recreation, or our parenting, we experience a kind of transcendence – episodes in which we lose awareness of time, and our other concerns fall away. When we attain this level of total preoccupation, the feeling of happiness is different. The 'pleasure' that accompanies 'flow' feels more profound than simpler forms of need-satisfaction.

---

[4] Csikszentmihalyi's research led him to believe that high levels of engagement with an activity for its own sake was conducive to thriving. In *'Flow: The Psychology of Optimal Experience'* (1990) he explained how intrinsic satisfaction can initiate an almost timeless experience in which all our energy and capability are focused on a problem or task, to the exclusion of everything else.

Generally speaking, the delight we experience in narrowing *the Gap* depends as much on anticipating the ideal as in our momentary glimpses of it. My wife loves to travel (I am writing this during the era of Covid-19, so this yearning is on pause right now). When her planning comes together, when we set off for distant destinations she has painstakingly scheduled, she is excitedly content, filled with the energy of expectancy. Yet so much of her happiness comes from the anticipation and preparation. When the cities and landmarks are visited, whether they are all that she expected or not is almost irrelevant. When we are back home again, it's not her recollections of the recent expedition alone that energise her, it is planning for the next!

It seems that this is another clue. Engagement - absorption in planning and achieving, being lost in the experience of putting together the pieces of some engrossing puzzle - all seem to be connected with thriving. This is the state that Csikszentmihalyi describes when he writes about 'flow'[5], the experience of being highly focused and engaged to the extent that nothing else seems to matter for that moment. Problems of the complexity that would otherwise be daunting are addressed and unravelled in the state of 'flow'.

As I sit sipping my coffee in Café Kirra, engrossed in my usual writing routine, I **could** bring many things to mind – especially ways in which my present experience does not match my ideal: my coffee has gone cold; I am struggling to find the right phrase; this chapter is taking much longer than I hoped it would; my back is aching; Covid-19 is still laying its dispiriting hand across my world so I can't travel, or go to work, or visit my grandchildren. Things are far from perfect! There are very definitely differences between my sense of the ideal and the world I am perceiving …. yet I find myself working with absolute contentment and no sense of effort. I am lost in what I am doing.

---

[5] Csikszentmihalyi concluded that the most profoundly satisfying and energising experiences occur in this state – so much so that he describes the 'flow' experience as the secret of happiness.

Happiness and the Good Life

In the face of the challenge of writing, and my absolute immersion in what I am doing, everything else fades from my awareness. Other pleasures seem irrelevant, and I ignore them. I easily forget the uncertainty and dismay that usually clatter noisily around the boundaries of my daily life. I am 'in the zone' - just as I was many years ago when I was running fast but without strain. It seems easy to thrive when this level of engagement is at the forefront of my attention.

Notice that being engaged in this way is also pleasurable. It's not completely unrelated to the first kind of happiness, but it feels infinitely more significant; intrinsic satisfaction that exists at the level of our deepest values. When we are in the 'flow' state, whatever we are engaged with seems supremely important.

However, there are three very individual variables which attend this second version of the happy life:
1. What we are engaged with must be something in our personal ideal world - the pursuit of some aspect of our own benchmark of Quality, arising from one of the reference points that we have established for ourselves. We don't experience 'flow' with anything we regard as uninteresting or insignificant. Personal autonomy, the pursuit of a goal that is intrinsically satisfying (never externally dictated), seems to be a necessary aspect of the 'flow' experience. We can't set up 'flow' for other people; they have to find it for themselves.
2. Whatever we are striving for should feel attainable. There must be a balance between the skills and capabilities we bring to our striving and *the Gap* we are trying to close. The personal competence that we bring to the challenge must be sufficient for the situation we are facing. One study[6] showed that if the perceived problem exceeds our capability, the result is stress, not 'flow'.
3. Achieving 'flow' requires not only a willing commitment, but also a thoughtful arrangement of circumstances. Distractions, such as

---

[6] J. Nakamura 'Flow Theory and Research' 2009: "Experiencing flow is about balancing the level of skill with the size and complexity of the challenge."

the intrusion of our mobile phones, interrupt 'flow'. So do self-criticism and doubt. Establishing a 'flow' state includes a commitment to self-management.

A Meaningful Life

There seems to be a connection between the first two kinds of happiness. Both the attainment of pleasure for its own sake (the pleasant life), and the pleasure that comes from engagement with something need-satisfying (as in 'flow'), seem to be related - although the pleasures feel very different.

The meaningful life appears to stand in contrast to these. Indeed, Victor Frankl[7] wrote explicitly: "Man's main concern is not to gain pleasure or to avoid pain but rather to seek a meaning in his life."

With the introduction of the 'meaningful life' as a possible third nutrient of our own capacity to thrive, we seem to have almost shifted from the realm of psychology to the domain of philosophy. Indeed, it was the existentialist philosopher Jean-Paul Sartre[8] who observed that every human being is responsible for working out their identity and their life's meaning, through the interaction between themselves and their environment. Is this a life-task that we must accept if we want to thrive?

Frankl certainly believed that his insight was psychological. He was convinced that the quest for the meaning and purpose of life is a symptom of a 'genetic restlessness' that affects most people. He developed 'logotherapy' to assist individuals to make the transition from a self-focused life to a life in which **meaning** is the focus. He argued that

---

[7] Victor Frankl was a survivor of the World War 2 death camps and the founder of logotherapy. In *'Man's Search for Meaning'* 1946, he describes his survival experience and how this led him to the belief that all humans strive for meaning. Frankl believed that having a purpose for his own life enabled him to survive the incredible privations of a death camp.
[8] Jean-Paul Sartre: *'Being and Nothingness'* 1956.

Happiness and the Good Life

discovering meaning - a purpose greater than our own survival and achievement - was necessary for human happiness. Hypothesising that all humans seek meaning to complete their sense of being whole, Frankl put forward the proposition that without this search all humans will experience tedium and frustration.

If we accept the postulate that a meaningful life is the third dimension of well-being, a life in which we can truly thrive, then the extra dimension seems to come from harnessing our ability to put together a story of our life in a way that frames and embraces the first two kinds of happiness.

Finding a narrative arc for our lives that goes beyond our own pleasure and competence, beyond the experience of need-gratification, is not brain activity; it takes us into the exclusive principality of the mind.

That we exist is a given. That we have genetic needs and that our brain is 'wired' to satisfy them is also a given. This is how the brain of the human control system works, varying little from that of a more primitive creature.

Working out who we are and what we are here for is not a given. We can only discover this for ourselves through the agency and creativity of consciousness.

Because our mind - the conscious product of our unconscious brain - has the capacity to surpass *the compass* of its origin, it is the mind alone that can grapple with meaning. The metacognitive capability it provides - the ability to observe and adjust our brain in action - can develop a narrative that makes sense of the choices we make and the impact that they have on the world around us. The connections in our brain may be linked by the axons of eighty-six billion neurons. Our thoughts and feelings are connected by the story that we tell ourselves about the purpose of our life.

Perceiving ourselves as having a meaningful life embraces the sense that we are in the service of a cause that is greater than personal survival and contentment. This sounds deeply spiritual - and it can be. It might embrace devotion to a deity or to a noble cause. Or it may be as simple as attempting to enrich the lives of others that we touch, or the belief that we are leaving an imprint on the world that is ours alone to make.

However small our legacy, it is ours to leave! We might share, with the author of Middlemarch[9], the idea that: "The growth of good in the world is partly dependent on un-historic acts." We do not have to be renowned to thrive!

Just as every life is distinctive, so are the parts we play and the differences we make. Every person can make a contribution of a scope and nature that is exclusive to their own life and circumstances. To paraphrase the Russian poet Yevgeny Yevtushenko: 'All people are interesting; as distinctive as the planets in the universe. Nothing in us is not exceptional; our existence is both personal and unique.'[10]

It's because we have this private access to the only mind that we will ever know that we inherit the responsibility to exercise its unique capacity, and to discover the purpose for our own life. As Sartre implies: 'If not us, then who?'.

---

[9] From the concluding lines of 'Middlemarch' by George Eliot, 1872.
[10] From 'People' by Yevgeny Yevtushenko: "No people are uninteresting / Their fate is like the history of planets / Nothing in them is not particular /and planet is dissimilar from planet / To each his world is private / and in that world one excellent minute / and in that world one tragic minute / These are private."

Twenty

Ingredients of 'the Good Life'

I am going to suggest that, in addition to the 'three kinds of happy' discussed in the previous chapter, there are seven other nutrients that may contribute to well-being; conditions that may help us to thrive. I present them for your consideration in no particular order. I don't suggest that all are 'requirements', only that these may be part of the patchwork of ingredients that contribute to our flourishing as individuals:

1. Outlook on adversity: thriving despite ….
2. Accepting of the challenge of *the Gap*.
3. A realistic but optimistic attitude.
4. Approach motivation.
5. Self-acceptance.
6. Compassion for others.
7. Choosing to look for ways to thrive.

Thriving despite.......

There is evidence that overcoming challenge - thriving 'despite' the difficulty of the times and events that we encounter - is important for our well-being. Victor Frankl suggested that encounters with adversity may actually be one of the pathways to a meaningful life. He maintained that although suffering itself is meaningless, our response to the experience gives it meaning.

We can thrive in spite of our actual life rarely matching the ideal. Disappointment is a normal life experience. Resilience defines the ability of the organism to bounce back from adversity. Thriving is the predisposition to seek a higher bounce. When we are thriving, we can not only recover from hardship, but we can also learn and grow from it. We invest what we learn in personal growth. As Nietzsche[1] suggested, that which does not damage us strengthens us.

Even if we reject the idea that an encounter with painful events may be a pre-requisite for thriving, we should at least consider the notion that good fortune need not be required for a happy and fulfilling life. I often think of my father's garden as a metaphor for the idea that we survive despite some level of hardship - although not necessarily because of it.

My father loved his garden. However, I would hesitate to call him a gardener! Our family's favourite cartoon was of an elderly gentleman reclining in a deck chair, immersed in reading a gardening magazine. Beside him a mountainous stack of similar magazines waited to be read. Around him was an erratic wilderness, waiting for the gardener's attention. That was Dad!

Despite his lack of systematic attention to them, his flowers and vegetables often flourished. Between the brambles and the wild grasses, flowers would proliferate and bloom. Although he would carelessly plant his seedlings in poorly prepared soil, an abundance of food sprung from his greenhouse. His garden thrived despite his neglect of it.

---

[1] Friedrich Nietzsche: "That which does not kill us makes us stronger" – a maxim from 'The Twilight of the Idols', 1889.

Ingredients of the Good Life

This may be an affront to everyday wisdom. It's commonly held that both plants and people are dependent on their surroundings - that both need the circumstances of living to be favourable in order to thrive. But wildflowers bloom in the rockiest soil, and human resilience and character are more likely to emerge from difficulty than from ease.

Although it's agreeable when things go well, it's something to be thankful for but not expect. Our inner world creates its own balance with the outer world, a balance that does not orbit around comfort alone. Thriving does not require favourable circumstances or desirable life events.

In fact, because *the Gap* between perfection and our predicament is always with us, perhaps we do only thrive 'despite' the problems that we face and learn from - at every step of our lives.

When we are thriving, it seems that we learn to measure our contentment on the barometer of the weather inside, not the drizzle on the outside. Thriving is not something that happens only when the stars align and *the Gap* appears to be closing; it's a feature of a frame of mind that is focused on what it can control, not what it can't.

Perhaps that is it! Perhaps it is our attitude to the reality of daily experience juxtaposed with the motives that urge us on (and not the nature of the circumstances themselves) that enable us to thrive.

Accepting the Challenge of *the Gap*

One recent study[2] that examined the meaning and experience of 'thriving' concluded that it was an amalgam of development and success. This links two themes which are common in many discussions about thriving: on the one hand, development, growth or flourishing[3]; on the other hand, actual success, or achievement. These motifs embrace both the experience of

---

[2] 'Human Thriving': Brown, Arnold, Fletcher and Standage, 1969.
[3] See for example the publications of Maslow, Deci and Ryan, Seligman.

'flow' and the achievement of an intrinsic goal, leaving open the question about which of these aspects of experience is more important. Is it the success or the struggle to succeed that feels like thriving?

I think of it like this: as similar to the experience of many an Olympic athlete. The dream of winning a gold medal, or a place in the final, or maybe just being selected for the Games, sustains their motivation for many years. Each successive achievement that brings them closer to their goal energises them with glimpses of dream fulfilment. The 'Gold Medal' is an archetype of everyone's most precious 'quality world' picture: a shining 'want' that invigorates and sustains months and years of striving.

Suddenly, the contest for which they have prepared is over! For the majority of contenders, the best they can hope for is that they have performed well, perhaps better than ever before. For others, there is disappointment. Then there are the fortunate few with a medal worn with pride around their neck. Euphoria kicks in - the ideal is achieved. If they are lucky, that emotional state may be sustained through the applause and tributes of ensuing days or weeks; but no emotion lasts forever.

Sooner or later, whether they are medal winners or simply 'Olympians', they will all stand on the empty pavement of life and think: 'what next?'

We are all like that. Humans need a 'what next' to function optimally. Most of us discover that it is not the outer trappings of the shiny medal (or its equivalent in our ideal world) that bring contentment. It is the struggle, the motion and emotion of the inner journey, not its culmination alone, that satisfies. It's the dream that draws us on, but the journey that makes it satisfying. We are thriving when we are journeying!

Not many of us are Olympians, but their experience is a parable for our own. Whether we are striving for and achieving our own markers of success; looking forward to and actively working towards the ideal in our own lives (be it a home, travel, family, a relationship, or a position of power and influence) – these draw us on. They are all goals which depend on the

Ingredients of the Good Life

existence of *the Gap* to galvanise our efforts. Life has purpose when we have something to strive for.

The '*no Gap*' experience would be apathy, not contentment. Having nothing to draw us on - no motivation – would not be thriving. We need to live in *the Gap* to function. Living without a '*Gap*' to close would be beyond miserable. As some people dejectedly describe it, there seems to be 'nothing to live for'.

Realistic Optimism

At times it's easy to think that pessimism is justified. As I write, the pall of Covid-19 is still hanging over every country, multiplying the uncertainty that is a normal part of life. We are divided and confused by this unexpected hiatus in the human trajectory, of the expectations we had come to rely upon. Although plagues, like wars, are recurring scars on the history of humanity, we are still capable of being surprised at their appearance in our lives. People everywhere seem to have bought into a general gloom. They bemoan both local and international events over which they have no control. Bad things are happening to good people - as they always have! How can optimism be justified? What is the point in looking for diamonds in this desert?

And yet, I am an optimist. Not a head-in-the-clouds optimist, but a realistic one. It seems that I probably *learned* that propensity. The research and writing of Martin Seligman[4] revealed that the human disposition to be optimistic or pessimistic is learned. We can learn to be hopeful or helpless.[5] Seligman explained that these two orientations arise from the ways in

---

[4] Martin Seligman: 'Learned Optimism' 1995, and 'Flourish' 2011.
[5] In 'Learned Optimism' 1995, Martin Seligman described explanatory style as the way in which we habitually explain good and bad events to ourselves. The degree to which we regard events as permanent or pervasive, and the degree to which we take personal responsibility for them, are the variables that lead us to be optimistic or pessimistic.

which we describe the world to ourselves; how we explain the occurrence of good and bad events. If we change our explanatory habits, we can transform the way in which we see the world. Seligman asserted that **realistic optimism** is the most rewarding attitude for those who want to live a satisfying life. The realism is as important as the optimism.

Since *the Gap* is an abiding feature of life, it tends to be those who are both realistic and optimistic who thrive. The optimist in us hopes for the best. The realist deals with whatever happens. Optimistic realism keeps these two inclinations in balance.

Because we know that the ideal life where everything works out as we want it to is the stuff of fantasy, the pragmatism of the realist is salutary. Although the essence of human motivation is to close the divide between the ideal and the real as much as possible, the realist accepts that we can't narrow every *Gap*. If we resent our inability to achieve the 'perfect' life and achieve every aspect of our ideal, we will self-inflict pain. A 'Pollyanna' attitude that approaches everything with unrealistic optimism can be damaging because it constantly delivers disappointment. Realism keeps us grounded.

Hope is an important feature of the optimistic attitude. So long as hope attends our experience, we can thrive. Without hope, our experience changes. Motive is deflated by our perception of our relative helplessness. If what we want seems unattainable, if *the Gap* appears too intractable to close, it's hard to flourish.

Ironically, it is in the moments of 'darkness' that pragmatism steps mostly firmly on to the stage of our perceptual system. When pessimism threatens us, the pragmatist takes a whole-of-life perspective, recognising that 'this too shall pass'. Bad times are not permanent. The wheel of life turns, as it always does.

Through the myriad interactions of our nervous system we are enabled to think and learn, and to direct innumerable aspects of our own existence. The energy emanating from the connections between billions of specialised

Ingredients of the Good Life

cells endows us with the gift of consciousness: the ability to observe and direct the neural technology that guides the activity of the fragile human organism that we inhabit. We live an everyday miracle. Expecting that things will be perfect is a bridge too far!

This equilibrium between pragmatism and hope supports our resilience. Perhaps it is the acquisition of this balance, the acceptance that the reality we are always weighing against the ideal is inevitably blemished, that frees us to thrive.

Our optimism reassures us that we can find ways in which to satisfy our needs; our realism reminds us not to depend on this!

Approach Motivation

Thriving is almost certainly related to the way we choose to manage *the Gap*, the attitude we take to the ever-present space between the apparent reality and our inner ideal.

In Chapter Eleven, I described the two kinds of motivation. One is the kind that recruits our behaviours in the service of improving our lives by achieving or approximating at least some of the aspirations of a life well lived. With this 'approach motivation' we enlist our mental and physical resources to attain what we desire.

The contrast to this is avoidance motivation: the kind of motivation that is focused on protecting *the Gap* and preventing it from widening. With this kind of motivation, we tend to be perennially on the look-out for danger and to marshal our energy and resources in the avoidance of potential pain. We are inevitably reactive in this motivational mode: playing defence against the attacks of the encroaching world.

In an uncertain world in which we can control only our own behaviours, avoidance motivation is exhausting. All our efforts are focused on coping;

on enduring. With our need for survival dominating, our other needs are pushed to the side. This is a recipe for enduring dissatisfaction.

When we are thriving, we are moving towards what we want - we are not in avoidance mode. Thriving entails making progress, having a destination and a road by which to travel. Opting to pursue what we want rather than reacting to what we don't want is one of the key choices for those who want to enhance their well-being. When we are thriving, our mind's inclination is to close *the Gap* and accept the risk.

Accepting Self

Self-acceptance may also be a necessary requirement of the experience of thriving. Through the avenues of personal contentment runs the thread of love – both for ourselves and for others. Thriving is incompatible with either self-criticism or intolerance.

Our mental preoccupation with *the Gap* can work against our self-esteem. Because we create an ideal, a quality picture of ourselves, it's impossible to ever match that perfect self for more than fleeting moments. Any time we do feel close to our ideal self we push our expectations further away and ask even better of ourselves. It's the personal treadmill, the urge to raise the bar with every increment of achievement.

We can be like athletes achieving a 'personal best', and then immediately setting a higher goal. That can be a healthy paradigm for self-improvement, except when **not** achieving the new standard becomes a self-critical measure. Like many an ageing athlete who won't let go of what is no longer possible, the increasingly remote ideal is harmful when it no longer draws us on but becomes the cross on which we hang our sense of relative failure or decline. The fading capacity of the former athlete is a paradigm for many mental health problems.

Knowing both the strengths and limitations of how our mind and brain manage *the Gap* can help us to be gentle with our imperfections. When we

Ingredients of the Good Life

understand how *the Gap* is created, we can see clearly how to use it for motivation but learn to reject it as a tool of self-criticism. To invert Nietzsche's aphorism, that which does not strengthen us may destroy us - unless we are gentle with ourselves

Unless we can come to terms with the limitations of being a self-created person, to love both what we have become and are becoming, it's difficult to thrive. Because we mentally embrace the images and conceptions of perfect quality that are the drivers of our approach motivation, we would be wise to avoid holding ourselves to an unforgiving standard. Minding *the Gap* describes the human journey: closing every divide is not an attainable destination!

Compassion

If we can accept and be sanguine about our own flaws, we are encouraged to be positive about the imperfections of others. Humans are, after all, both the minders of a mental life and the instruments of an animated brain. Expecting perfection from anyone is to assume that our species has a degree of self-management that is beyond the capacity of the human control system. We are all flawed. Refusing to be reconciled to this will not only slam the doors of self-acceptance, but also turn off the taps of compassion and empathy for others.

'Flawed' people are like painful events[6]. They intrude upon the even tenor of our way, creating circumstances beyond our control. We don't choose our unsettling encounters with people, but the degree to which they disturb us is ours to control. We can exercise self-discipline even if we can't

---

[6] This is an expression of my realism. Knowing that all humans choose their pathways to need-satisfaction, which can sometimes be found in wicked places, is part and parcel of our understanding of the brain and mind. There are nefarious choices, and we all have the potential to be malevolent. Fortunately, it's not the mainstream of human development. We can't ignore the existence of personal flaws, but neither should our attitudes to other people be shaped around our fear of it.

control the situation. If I choose not to be vexed by the lack of consideration, rudeness or even malice of other people, I am making choices for the only person I can control. As Frankl reminded us, the ultimate human freedom is to choose our own way in the face of adversity.

Research shows us that compassion is one of the triune dimensions of resilience.[7] Bereft of the ability to accept and forgive, it's hard to flourish. Resentments and dislikes tie our equanimity too closely to the capriciousness of other people.

Like us, other people are imperfect and are sometimes damaged by their own choices. When we know and accept the nature of our humanity - the gift of an amazing but wilful brain from which emanates a sometimes-unreliable mind - we can learn not to be too inflexible with ourselves or with other people.

The mind is the slower dimension of our control system. It enables us to make reflective decisions instead of snap judgments. It can offer us more deliberate and helpful options in its own slightly ponderous time - but it's lazy! Our constructed mind can serve us magnificently when we discipline its musings. Left alone, it often simply goes along with the swift approximations of the 'hustling' brain.

Knowing and accepting these limitations of our control system helps us to thrive. We can ignore the distractions of imperfection and use them as a lever for our own learning and growth.

Thriving is an active choice

Thriving requires us to be active: it implies doing. Its synonyms such as flourishing, growing, progressing, making progress are verbs. There is a

---

[7] According to Boyatzis and McKee: 'Resonant Leadership' 2005 - the three dimensions of resilience are hope, compassion and mindfulness.

Ingredients of the Good Life

sense of motion involved in thriving. It's deliberate, not contingent. It's hard to imagine thriving by accident.

Across the boundary that separates activity and passivity, the mental states that accompany these poles of experience stare at each other across an emotional chasm. On the one hand there are striving, thriving, extending, learning, and growing. On the other hand there are surviving, enduring, hanging on, and existing. The difference between them is not the degree of effort or persistence. Both of these are often required whether we are flourishing or just existing. The distinguishing feature of a thriving state seems to be whether we are purposeful in seeking to procure and sustain our own well-being.

Most of us wish to thrive. We would rather be flourishing than feeling that we are drifting towards stagnation. However, thriving depends upon our will to act. Wishing it is not enough. The pursuit of a life state in which we can be described as flourishing involves the active accumulation of positive habits. Neither the labyrinthine brain nor the deliberative mind can take us directly to that desirable place. Choosing to thrive is an elaborate compilation of decisions: not one choice but many, yet all based on the predisposition to learn, adapt, accept, and evolve.

From a brain perspective, it never could be one choice. The brain doesn't work like that. We don't have one neural network that manages everything and that pivots on a single coordinated set of synaptic connections. In our sensible moments, we realise that we can't hold more than a few things in our mind at once. Making and enacting a single all-encompassing decision about our well-being and personal growth is beyond us. To thrive we must make many choices.

Yet there is a commonality about the choices that lead to a thriving life: a pervasive willingness to be open to both possibility and pain in order to exploit the choices presented to us by our cognition.

Not only is thriving constructed from a multiplicity of choices, it is itself multi-faceted. In the pages of this book I have been interchanging terms like well-being, contentment, satisfaction, resilience, and flourishing - and relating them to our ability to thrive. I know that there are differences between these emotional states. I have linked them because they are related in life, if not in the lexicon. Thriving is not exactly the same as well-being or resilience or deep contentment. Nevertheless, there are sufficient resemblances between them to believe that they come from the same family[8] of states of mind. Even if the words don't mean the same, they are analogous: containers into which we pour our personal conceptions of an ideal life.

We are most likely to thrive when we set out to do so - when we choose the intent to discover and explore avenues of well-being rather than settling for less. Knowing that it is possible to thrive, we can willingly explore the way in which the nutrients described in this chapter are encountered and explore them as fully as we can.

Committing ourselves to using our mind to govern our restless brain helps us to thrive. Paying attention to *the Gap* and learning from it, we become mindful. Becoming mindful, we manage our brain and mind so that these inseparable entities serve us well.

---

[8] Philosopher Ludwig Wittgenstein argued that words may not have exactly the same meaning or have everything in common, but they can be connected by 'family resemblances' - associations that link them to one another in many different ways. 'Philosophical Investigations (§65)' 1953

Minding the Gap

Twenty-One

Minding *the Gap*

Embracing the Mind's Gift

Our brains will run our lives, whether we like it or not! Like background music, ever-present but only occasionally noticed, the subliminal bustle along our neural pathways strives to keep us safe and to find ways to satisfy our needs. The brain's unconscious zeal prompts us to sustain ourselves and endure.

If we desire more of life than staying safe and surviving, we will be wise to explore the potential of the brain's slower faculty - the conscious processing capacity that we label 'mind'.

Paying attention to the processes of mind makes sense. After all, none of us would want to be described as a mindless person. We would not often choose to relinquish the steering wheel of our internal control system and cede command to the comparatively primitive impulses of the brain. Behaving mindlessly would be to surrender to the dictates of habit or whim. The preferable alternative is to be **mindful**, to mind our own motivation and behaviour through heedful thought.

Mindfulness, we might notice, has many patrons. Consequently, mindfulness is often construed as the property of a defined set of meditative activities, or a particular spiritual orientation. Within these disciplines there is often an emphasis on 'emptying the mind' in order to purify our thoughts.

I am **not** using the word mindful in that sense!

As I characterise it, mindfulness is not so much about clearing the mind as it is about paying close attention to its activity. We don't need to be devotees of the eight-fold path[1], practitioners of Hatha Yoga[2] or devoted to the daily practice of mediation to be my kind of mindful. I am referring to mindfulness in its plainest sense: as **paying attention to the activity of the mind and harnessing the mental activity we observe in the service of our well-being.** Mindfulness is good mind-management.

There are two critical practices required to execute this everyday kind of mind-management. They require us to be 'present-centred' and non-judgmental by:
1. Managing our attention so that it is focused on our immediate experience - on what's happening now. When we are attending in this way, we identify and focus on the mental events that are related to whatever is currently going on. At the same time, we deliberately dismiss thoughts about what is **not** happening now.
2. Suspending judgment about events as they occur gives our mind time to be curious. In this cognitive mode, we can allow ourselves to be accepting and open to new learning and resist the mind's tendency to make assumptions and jump to conclusions.

Managing our own mind in these two ways helps us to limit the volume of intrusive activity promoted by the automated brain.

---

[1] The fourth of the Buddha's four noble truths includes an eight-fold pathway to the transcendence of suffering and the achievement of insight.
[2] A Hindu practice involving both physical and mental self-discipline.

Minding the Gap

The Brain Connects and Distracts

The natural activity of our brain is to make connections. So, when an event or activity takes place which has possible implications for us, those brain circuits with associations to that event offer us information - whether or not it is relevant or helpful. This crackle of synaptic suggestions can easily overwhelm the slower ruminations of consciousness - unless they are managed.

Let's paint a scenario. Say that towards the end of a busy but rewarding day one of my trusted colleagues hints that he may soon resign and look for another job. This is just information. Like all data that is received by our sensory system, I process it internally, I interpret it.

There are two ways in which I can mentally process the information:
1. If I am mindful, I will notice what is happening in my brain. I will identify the jolt of anxiety that I feel, accept it - and let it go. Knowing that my brain is liable to build on the anxiety if I attend to it, I manage my own thinking. I choose not to pursue it. Staying in the present, I understand that there is nothing I need to do in the immediate moment - except perhaps express my concern and support for my colleague: 'Is he OK? Does he need help from me?'. I let him know how much I have valued working with him. This is all that's required in the moment. I am managing my mind and choosing a response that is immediately relevant.
2. Alternatively, I can surrender to the tumult of my unmanaged mental activity. I can allow my brain circuitry to embark on a speculative journey, a narrative constructed from abundant fragments of past experience and prevailing fears. I can begin to wonder when he will leave and what that will mean to me. I allow myself to ruminate about who will replace him, what their skills might be, whether it will mean extra work for me. I think about the possible challenges ahead, how my seniority may be questioned, the risk that the personality of the new person might make work more difficult for me. I remember working with other

people who were uncooperative and the unpleasantness which that entailed. I recall difficult conversations I have had with those other people and begin rehearsing such a conversation in my head, dreading the potential outcome. I am thinking about how unhappy I may be and whether I should myself quit this job in order to avoid all this future difficulty – *which, by the way, has not happened. It's in my imagination* ! My unmanaged brain has simply taken the kernel of anxiety that I felt and let it rip!

Our brain amplifies our anxieties quite naturally. Without mindful self-management, it can blur present with past and future to create scenarios full of distraction or dread.

When I am consciously managing my mind, knowing the dance of the brain and mind, I can choose to let the mind lead. Responding mindfully, focusing only on what is happening here and now, I can manage the situation without gathering and feeding the momentum of potential stress.

The mind commonly presents us with choices like this: choices between attending to the immediate or being distracted by its implications. Sitting on a beach on a summer's day I can allow myself to simply soak up the pleasure of the sun's warmth, the soothing of the sea breeze, the rhythm of the breaking waves. I can pay attention to these pleasures and enjoy them, choosing to ignore the relentless associations presented on the fringes of consciousness by the connective brain. I can banish the intrusive reminders that the holiday is nearly over, that difficulties loom at work, or that this is the season of impending cyclones, bush fires and floods. All these may lurk in the future, but they are not happening at the moment.

It is not easy to remain present-centred and ignore these distractions. Choosing to manage our mind does not banish these intrusions from knocking on the door of our awareness. The warnings and memos from our brain will still trespass into the portals of consciousness. However, choosing to be mindful, we can imagine these unwanted thoughts as if they were bubbles rising from the ocean floor.

Minding the Gap

Generated from the depths of our unconscious, fragments of thought may bubble into our consciousness, but we can use our imagination to manage them. We can visualise them as vague forms rising unexamined through the mind and disappearing into the vast clear sky above the surface of awareness. Or we can imagine these associations as whirling on the rim of a wheel that spins around us while we remain in the stillness of the hub[3], choosing to notice only the people and events that we can influence in the present.

Minding the Neural Network

The brain is, by design, a prolific networker. It makes connections even when we don't want or need them. Sometimes these connections may fill our head with 'what might happen' and 'what else should I have done?' - thoughts that interfere with our well-being. That's why we often need to be mindful managers of where our brain is taking us. We can save ourselves a great deal of distress by learning how to control the tendency of the brain's networks to present the same perceived threat repeatedly.

Whenever we identify something that is a potential threat to our well-being, the brain alerts the connections that trigger the 'anxiety circuits'.[4] Anxiety is a protective measure; it is important that we notice potential danger. It feels unpleasant but it serves its purpose. However, when the threat is **not** in the present but is future speculation or a fragment of past experience, the brain sends alerts anyway. These repeated reminders are like the messages that pop up in your inbox reminding you 'just in case'

---

[3] 'The wheel' is a powerful strategy embedded in a metaphor suggested by Dan Siegel.
[4] I am using the term 'anxiety circuits' as a generalisation for the many brain circuits that assess and address our fears. Sometimes there is too much activity in brain areas that detect threat; at other times there is too little activity in areas that are designed to modulate it. Occasionally the connections between related brain areas are overactive. All of these potential sources of stress can be managed to some degree by mindful re-direction.

you had forgotten something. They are irritating. They might be an aid to memory, but they generate unwanted emotion.

The problem occurs when the 'memo from the brain' triggers the same anxiety circuits whenever it occurs. The brain does not know whether the feared event is imminent or not; it is a secluded container that only has access to danger through our internal processing. Every time the fear 'comes to mind' it summons anxiety. We call this 'worrying'. The fear trigger for the anxiety keeps occurring because we keep presenting it to ourselves. The thought may relate to external events, but worry is generated inside us. Like all the brain's activity it can all too easily become a habit.

A managed mind deals with this anxiety in a timely manner. Mindful understanding of what is happening enables us to exert conscious control over the brain's automated memos. Remember that the mind **does** have the capacity to modify the brain's activity.

As anyone who is often anxious knows, it's not enough to simply think (or be told) 'stop worrying'. The mind can't process this negative. What's needed instead is something to replace the worry - something else to think or do. Mind management often involves some combination of:

- Noticing the mental activity that is occurring in the present moment.
- Confronting the thoughts that are creating the anxiety and realising that they are mental events we can control.
- Challenging the consequences that we are predicting.
- Reinterpreting the perception that is generating the fear.
- Paying attention to something different.
- Choosing to take actions that will change the physiology of anxiety.

Mindfulness can shield us through knowledge and self-discipline. Knowing clearly what is happening in our thinking enables us to calm the fear. Realising that our brain is simply sending us memos *feels* very different from reacting to persistent fear.

Having learned that there are many ways to manage our mind in dealing with these situations, we can summon our repertoire of alternative behaviours with which to challenge the unwanted thoughts.

I tend to be very direct with my internal control system. I talk to myself.[5] I might say: "Thanks brain, I don't need you." Quite often I ask myself: "Can I do anything about this situation right now? If not, what can I do instead?"

We all do talk to ourselves all the time, but often we do not manage the conversation well. Being clear and firm with our internal communication – as if we were talking assertively to someone else – is an effective way of sending messages to the unconscious.

Among a host of other strategies that can be used to help manage anxious or repetitive thinking are:
- Noticing what the brain is doing and deliberately ignoring it by switching our attention to something different.
- Practising the ABCDE technique of Cognitive Behaviour Therapy.[6]
- Imagining a bubble forming around the unwanted thoughts and blowing them away.
- Asking ourselves: "What am I doing? Is it helping? What else can I do?"

---

[5] We all talk to ourselves. It's an internal dialogue that is part of healthy mental functioning. However, our internal chatter can be helpful or harmful. Choosing to talk sense to yourself is helpful.
[6] Albert Ellis developed the ABCDE process to help people notice and challenge their anxious or depressing beliefs about an event. His process involves noticing the activating event (A) and confronting the belief (B) that generates the anxiety, recognising the harmful consequence (C) of associating the event and the belief, and disputing (D) the relevance or usefulness of the belief in order to arrive at more effective (E) beliefs and thoughts.

- Taking at least 10 deep breaths, fully exhaling before each new inhalation. As we exhale, breathe out unwanted thoughts.
- Doing some exercise with as much intensity as possible.
- Focusing our attention on something that can be accomplished straight away.
- Summoning a humorous image of fighting off a horde of unwanted thoughts.
- Hearing the 'voice' that keeps intruding into your thoughts and changing its tonalities to those of a favourite cartoon character.

Some of these seem fairly eccentric! However, they all require deliberate changes in thinking, so they do serve our purpose - they increase our control over our mind. None of them is a one-off strategy. They work best when we practise until they become habits. Worrying itself becomes a habit if we don't manage it and replace it with more useful routines.

The Rewards of a Managed Mind

Mindfulness rewards us in spades. It allows us to deal with the inevitable problems and uncertainties of living only when they happen; when the problem actually occurs. The restless connectivity of the brain offers us the same problem repeatedly – in multiple agonies of anticipation and endless brooding re-runs! We can be fated to deal with challenging circumstances or demanding people over and over again, instead of once.

Of course, paying attention mindfully does not seal us off from healthy planning or from heading off impending problems. This is indeed where paying attention to what the mind is doing pays off for us. We learn how to identify the difference between circumstances that should be dealt with immediately, and those which we can safely ignore until they eventuate. We can deal with setbacks when they happen, rather than do this every time that fear of them drifts through the circuits of our perceptual system.

Minding the Gap

As we learn to pay attention to own internal control system, we can more easily understand and manage the impulses that are generated by the vast array of binary switches in our brain. Mindfulness is the ability to filter our own perceptions and attend to what matters when it matters. It allows us to see things as they are **now**, without the preconceptions and memories that cling to the coattails of perception like a fretting child.

Understanding that the brain in trying to protect us can often overwhelm us, we can firmly calm its activity. Adopting a mindful perspective, we can take the observer role, the Third Perceptual Position[7], and make our choices from that vantage point. Paying attention in this way encourages our mind to zoom out of the state of mental confusion and view ourselves from an observer perspective.

Managing our mental life has many benefits.[8] It is stress-reducing; it enables us to feel more capable - and less reactive. When we are regulating our thinking, we can step off the racetrack of whirling thoughts and deal with things one at a time. The self-managed mind knows that multi-tasking is a harmful illusion[9], and that working within the attentional capacity of the mind enables us to be calm and composed. The mindful approach enables us to 'keep our head when all around us are losing theirs and blaming it on us!' [10]

---

[7] Third Perceptual Position is the practice of focusing our attention as if we are observers of our own thoughts and actions rather than participants in them. Based on ideas from Gregory Bateson and Virginia Satir, the Perceptual Positions are commonly used in psychology and Neuro-linguistic Programming. Third Perceptual Position is a surprisingly easy strategy to learn.

[8] See Keng, Smoski and Robins: 'The Effects of Mindfulness on Psychological Health: A Review of Empirical Studies' in 'The Clinical Psychology Review ' 2011. They concluded that "Mindfulness brings about various positive psychological effects, including increased subjective well-being, reduced psychological symptoms and emotional reactivity, and improved behavioural regulation."

[9] The mind can only pay attention to one thing at a time. We can of course switch our attention rapidly back and forth. However, this is tiring and erodes concentration. G. Zauberman: 'The Illusion of Multi-Tasking', 2017.

[10] An adapted fragment from the poem 'If' by Rudyard Kipling.

Mind-Managing *the Gap*

Managing our own mind bring us two perspectives: both a generic knowledge of how the brain and the mind operate within the human control system, and the ability to pay specific attention to the working of the only mind we can ever truly know - the one embedded within us.

The Gap juxtaposes our perception of the world with the wants that we pursue in order to satisfy our needs. Our minding of this divide is a three-fold act of self-governance:
1. One the one hand, we can manage our **perceptions** by understanding that they are our own interpretations.
2. On the other hand, we can choose the way we **present our 'ideal' to ourselves**. From our accumulated picture-book of 'wants' we can choose those which draw us on without discouraging us.
3. Between these two elements of the dichotomy, we can choose the **ways** in which we satisfy our needs.

Knowing that we have this trinity of options for minding our *Gaps* enables us to refine our motivation. We can deepen our understanding of *the Gap* and employ this triad of mindful strategies in ways that helps us to thrive.

Minding ourselves encourages us to be wary of the restless tendencies of our unconscious activity. The brain can fritter away its massive processing power in snatching at momentary pleasures or guarding us against imaginary threats. Thankfully, the reflective mind can slow and re-direct these impulses. When we pay attention to the mind's activity, our slower thinking can guide the brain by aligning it with purposeful intention.

Our unconscious processing knows nothing of meaning and purpose; it has no long-term plans for us. It's our capacity for consciousness, the reflective capability of mind, that gives human thriving the extra dimension that will promote our need-satisfaction to a higher level.

Twenty-Two

A Meaningful Life

The Construction of Meaning

We need the capacities of mind to direct our lives purposefully and to discover meaningful ways to live. That's what the conscious mind can do, but the unconscious activity of the brain cannot.

So far as we know, finding and then living in accord with a purpose higher than our own comfort is a uniquely human characteristic. It does not naturally emerge from the synaptic searching of the unconscious. Formulating meaning in our lives requires the ability to reflect and to self-evaluate, to perceive a pattern to our life and to ask ourselves if we are following it.

The study of being and identity, which once seemed to belong to philosophy, has now been embraced by neuroscientific research. It appears that there are features of our brain function that steer us to define ourselves individually, and that doing so contributes strongly to our sense of well-being.

We are more likely to thrive when we identify a meaning for our lives; when we make sense of where our choices have taken us and where we want to direct our future energy.

The search for meaning stretches back into history. The travellers who came from afar to consult the oracle in ancient Delphi often hoped that they would receive profound insights with which to guide their lives and predict their future. However, from what we infer from the first inscription in the forecourt of the Temple of Apollo, they often left with a single fragment of universal wisdom: 'Know thyself'.

The counsel of the Delphic Oracle applies to us as surely as to the ancient Greeks. If we want to make sense of our life, we must look within, to allow our mind to seek and recognise the unfolding elements of our own story. The tracks of our life history tell us about the events and intentions that have energised us, and those that have depleted us. From this information, we can examine the relationships between the two in order to work out who we are and what we are here for.

The 6th Century philosopher Boethius[1] was uncomfortably direct in his assessment of those who do not acquaint themselves with self-knowledge, writing that "Lack of self-knowledge is natural in other living creatures, but in humans it is a moral blemish."

Self-awareness precedes the emergence of meaning.

Meaning is etymologically as well as practically connected to mind.[2] It denotes the mind's capacity to search for reasons; for why our life is significant. When we direct our mind to our awareness of self and search through the annals of our personal history, we quite naturally select the

---

[1] Anicius Manlius Severinus Boethius (c. 480- 524 CE) is best known for his influential work 'The Consolation of Philosophy'.
[2] Old English 'mænan' is related to the Dutch 'meenen' from an Indo-European root 'shared by mind'.

A Meaningful Life

features of our past that seem most likely to help us steer the future. From these threads, we weave a pattern of 'meaning'.[3]

We can identify our purpose in life[4] by taking the time to understand the way in which our distinctive mind assigns value. We know ourselves best when we are clear about the beliefs that we have developed and the ways we have put these into practice. To accomplish those insights, we can ask these questions of ourselves:
— *What energises me?*
— *What am I naturally inclined to do with no urging or effort?*
— *What depletes me? What do I avoid?*
— *What is my attitude to 'the Gap'?*
— *What is so valuable to me that I cannot let it go?*
— *What am I proud of?*

As we put together our answers to those questions, we can add to them everything else that we have discovered about our personality and our genetic predispositions. Learning about the way in which our mind works, incorporating our personality preferences and our cultural biases, we construct meaning for ourselves. Meaning is inevitably constructed; it is not inherited or discovered.

From self-knowledge, we can begin to assemble our answers to the question: "What does it mean to be me?". Asking ourselves questions such as these may help us to find the pattern of meaning in which to entrust our future:
— *Who am I? How do I describe myself to myself?*

---

[3] I am choosing to discount the 'meaning' that is prescribed by religion. Firstly, because this kind of 'meaning' is usually accompanied by commands - which are anathema to our life-affirming need for autonomy. Secondly, because I think it empirically unlikely that a deity who created such diverse beings would impose a 'one-size-fits-all' solution to the human search for meaning.
[4] Purpose in Life is a current area of neuro-psychological research. Studies show that those who have identified their own 'purpose in life' are more resilient and more likely to thrive as they age than those who are not purpose-driven: Kaplan and Anzaldi 'Purpose Driven Life' – Cerebrum 2015:7th edition.

- *What is the contribution I make, or could make?*
- *What is more important to me than success?*
- *What do I want to be known for?*

With these questions we examine the autobiographical self, the sense of identity that seems to be uniquely human. It is this perception of our individuality that allows us to create a narrative arc for our own life, an internal awareness that tells us the story of who we are and what we are here for.[5]

Within this sense of self is forged an unbreakable connection between identity and purpose, between how we see ourselves and what we believe to be meaningful for us.

Both who we are and what we regard as significant in our lives flow down through the logical (and perhaps neuro-logical) levels of our mental processing into our behaviours.[6]

We are constructed from our responses to experience and are always searching for what is most important to us. We face the volatile circumstances of our life and behave in ways that bring both a sense of control and a feeling of progress to our circumstances. We subsequently choose to acquire the capabilities that support these behaviours.

As we mature and learn, adapting to the triumph and tedium that are the inevitable accompaniments of a human life, we consciously respond in harmony with the person we have become. Once developed, our identity and purpose flow back into our behaviours. We pursue what we value.

---

[5] This is congruent with the view of self that is proposed by Anthony Damasio. Damasio describes 'self' as the enduring aspect of consciousness, the subjective perspective that is central to having a mind. He argues that because the master map of self is sourced from within our own body, it is our key interpreter of all the other perceptual maps which we create to represent 'reality' to ourselves. Anthony Damasio: 'Self Comes to Mind', 2010.

[6] As predicted by Robert Dilts' explanation of Logical Levels: 'A brief History of Logical Levels', Robert B Dilts, 2014.

A Meaningful Life

Our actions are shaped by what we believe about the behaviours that will both satisfy our needs and take us ever closer to the person we would like to be.

Another way of explaining this is to view our 'self', which is the enduring consciousness of our body and its orientations, as if it were a master map through which we interpret all the other maps[7] that we create in order to make sense of the world. Subsequently, as we connect our daily thoughts and actions with the identity that we form within ourselves, we experience a sense of coherence and personal authenticity which calms our inner restlessness. Frankl described this as one of the essentials of a meaningful life, living in tune with our decisions about how life should be.

When we take responsibility for living out the behaviours that emerge from who we are, we experience what Frankl described as the 'freedom of the will'. Having discerned a purpose in our life, we can live authentically, faithful to the meaning that we have constructed for ourselves.

Authenticity feels right. Its opposite is an aimless life in which we fall into the trap of what Sartre describes as *bad faith:* an existence which is attended by self-deception and a sense of emptiness, because we have no meaning to turn to. *Bad faith* anchors us to the opinions of others and the fickle contortions of whatever compromise is socially acceptable or morally convenient. Conversely, *good faith* is the antithesis of the inauthentic – it's the sincere intent to be faithful to our own sense of purpose by making choices that are grounded in our self-perception. Being true to ourselves, we take responsibility for becoming the person we aspire to be - at one with our personal ideals and predictable to other people. When we live with this sense of authenticity, we are equipped to thrive.

---

[7] Alfred Korzybski, 'Science and Sanity', 1933.

The Thriving Mind

Because mind and brain are the conscious and unconscious faces of the same entity, it's difficult to talk about their different avenues of contribution without falling into the fallacy of dualism. I have been keen to avoid that. Throughout this book, I have stressed that mind and brain are one. However, recognising that they are dissimilar faces of the same entity, we can usefully notice and manage the ways in which they work in unison to create the control system that is a human entity.

Because every brain is uniquely formed, the myriad connections made within it are distinctively fashioned. They are wired together by the moments and memories that shape them, the problems encountered, the challenges faced. Similarly, the awareness that emerges from the brain's energy - that conscious inner perception that we call mind - is also individual. The patterns of mind are shaped by the brain from which they emanate. In its turn, the mind can modify the brain which is its origin.

We know that the brain is a physical structure that automates whatever we do and operates mostly outside of our conscious control. Its network of connections is well suited to habit.

When we need detached awareness, conscious inner perception of the brain's activity, we call on mind. What mind can do is bring the light of consciousness to the ceaseless interaction of our brain's synaptic activity. Activity in the concealed house of the brain is often only observable from its outputs as a human organism - from the behaviours that it directs. The mind affords us glimpses inside, as if leaking the light of awareness through the shutters of the brain's enclosure.

By choosing to notice the capacities of mind and manage these through awareness, reflection, self-knowledge, and self-evaluation, we can steer our lives to help ourselves to thrive.

A Meaningful Life

Although there is much that we can't do in the uncertain world that is the home of our body, we can be buoyed by the hope of what we **can do** and take delight in whatever we achieve.

Whether we flourish in the spotlight, or contentedly occupy our own quiet corner of the world, we can shape and mind the only life we will ever live. Although we may not predict or unfailingly control all the events of our life, it is in our grasp to design who we want to be and to actively pursue the ideals that draw us on to be that person.

Because we know that the restless brain does not provide us with a purpose beyond the satisfaction of needs, we are liberated to find our own reason for being through our conscious musing. The mind's reflective capacity, its ability to float free of its sensory origins and search for explanation, enables us to find meaning in life. Wherever the journey of inner exploration takes us, we can find joy in the road travelled.

The conviction that learning enriches us through pain as readily as through gladness may be a hallmark of the ability to thrive. We thrive despite the deserts and chasms, not because we scale the peaks but because we resolutely steer towards them. As Nietzsche observed: "When we have a WHY to live, we can bear almost any HOW."

The circumference of human knowledge always prowls on the boundary of an infinity of ignorance. What we don't yet know and understand steers us towards hope: the belief that sparks of promise and potential will be lit from the transient embers of our present experience.

Aware that everything we can control is within ourselves, we can choose our journeys and our destinations. We can be the authors of our own script; we can decide how to travel our difficult by-ways and choose again when the path is blocked. The brain may remain an organ of deep mystery but knowing something of the way it is harnessed to the mind to steer us, we can be cheerfully reconciled to the scenery it reveals.

Misunderstood, the profound mystery of mind has the capacity to cloak us in illusion and magnify our self-deception. We can make too much of our providential gift of awareness and muddle our living with humourless hubris. **Or** we can choose to be mindful! We can mind the self-deceptions that we easily create in ourselves and try to understand them. Coming to terms with our own awareness as being simply the energetic aura of a biological brain grounds and humbles us.

At birth, we are not given much! In essence, all we are is muscle, bone, connective tissue and organs, contained within a bag of skin, piloted by the vast accumulation of binary switches that we call our brain. That we can learn to transcend the bare biology of our being - that we can be of the same ilk as the great minds which conceived and created the heritage of humanity - is humbling and astonishing.

Because the patterns of our brain and the processes of our mind stamp us with uniqueness, we can evade the discouraging hand of limitation and offer our singular contribution to the possibilities created by the human organism.

Thriving is our sense that we have understood the potential of our lives, stared down its limitations and are determined to exploit the choices available to us. Like the voyage of a storm-tossed vessel, faltering at times in the grip of wind and tide, we can steer through uncertainties and make our heading resolutely in the face of unpredictable circumstances.

The satisfied life is not a spectator experience. None of us will flourish if we are living on the sidelines. Choosing to thrive in this uncertain world, we can unleash the processes of mind to address *the Gap* between perception and ideal, however great the obstacles.

Our life's purpose is not defined by comparison with others or by the achievement of conventional goals. Set against the immensity of the Universe and the brief span of a human existence, life is indeed simply what we make of it.

A Meaningful Life

At any instant, we can pause and take stock of the values that populate the equation of our lives: balancing the elements of our ideal word against the experiences that we would prefer to avoid. If we notice a disparity between what we aspire to and what we hold to be possible, we can take action to add value to our life. As long as we draw breath, we can choose to be purposeful in this way - to add to our stock of significant events and experiences by whatever small accumulations are possible.

This willingness to enhance ourselves gives direction to our odyssey through a meaningful life. Although it may not be our lot to 'slay dragons' or to have our achievements feted in the public sphere, facing the tribulations of life with acceptance, hope and perseverance is itself a kind of heroism. We are all capable of a life of daring: of opportunities seized and risks taken in the face of ever-present uncertainty. Like the heroes of mythology, we can be sustained by on our own journey and emerge liberated and ennobled by our achievements and contributions - whatever they may be!

Rob Stones
March 2022

www.ingramcontent.com/pod-product-compliance
Lightning Source LLC
Chambersburg PA
CBHW050311010526
44107CB00055B/2193